Blessings,
May the Lord be your guide!!
In Christ's Love,
Mary Lou

LET HIM REIGN

A MOTHER'S JOURNEY
FROM TRAGEDY TO
HOPE AND JOY

MARY LOU

Inspiring Voices®

Inspiring Voices books may be ordered through booksellers or by contacting:

Inspiring Voices
1663 Liberty Drive
Bloomington, IN 47403
www.inspiringvoices.com
1 (866) 697-5313

Scripture taken from the King James Version of the Bible.

ISBN: 978-1-4624-1283-9 (sc)
ISBN: 978-1-4624-1284-6 (e)

Library of Congress Control Number: 2019915017

Print information available on the last page.

Inspiring Voices rev. date: 10/29/2019

Dedication

In Loving Memory of my dear friend, Sellie

Introduction

In a world full of chaos and conviction, nothing on this earth could ever prepare me for the thralls of unexpected death. While everyone else's life marched on at full speed ahead, mine was abruptly interrupted with a major pitstop. Like the brakes that came screeching to an ear-piercing halt, so screamed my entire being, my entire soul. And with that, I was thrown off the main course on an endless road of time, leaving me at a stand still in mind, body, and spirit. I may have stopped quickly, however that was followed by a substantial tailspin, attaching my life to one extreme alteration off the course. Abandoning the assortment of colors that were familiar to me, I was shoved into a narrow tunnel, squeezing through and scraping off all remaining color to then be dropped into a place of total darkness. This is the true- life story of how I lost my son at the tender age of twenty-one. Wearing my heart out on a sleeve, raw and exposed to all, I share with you my journey of grief, offering nothing but truth and honesty in how I felt in those early moments and the ones that followed. I'm only human and I'm certainly not perfect so perhaps some words may sound repetitious while other emotions may seem extreme. Sadly, in all sincerity, there were strained relationships with some loved ones. My heart was torn to pieces. I had just had the most unexpected tragedy thrown my way, taking me on the ride of a lifetime. I have to say, I was shaken to the core and my entire body went into shock mode. Ultimately, I was struggling for survival and I couldn't possibly do this alone. Thankfully I reached out for the Hand of God.

Thank You, Lord, for bringing me on this journey of love lost, despair, and frustration, leading me back to a path of hope and love everlasting. I don't wish this mother's sorrow on any woman, but I can certainly sympathize and am so willing to share the journey of healing through one mother's nightmare — my own.

Monday, May 6th – the day that eternally changed my life

I was in the back section of the mail truck moving letters up front and rearranging packages when I received the phone call. It was my son-in-law Sean at the other end of the line telling me that he and my daughter Tiffany were on their way to New York. My son Matthew was in the hospital experiencing chest pains and he might need heart surgery. Oh, dear God! My heart broke. After hanging up, I sat there and cried. This is so messed up, because my son is only twenty-one years old and a healthy young man. Why was all of this happening? I don't understand. This is incomprehensible as well as entirely out of my control. Further, once I gathered up enough energy, I called the post office unaware of how inaudible my voice was to the receiver. After finally getting the words out, I went inside the small mailroom to accommodate the customers by sorting their correspondence. I was reassured by someone who had overheard my crying, saying that everything would be okay.

Okay... insert self-talk here... He's in the hospital but he's healthy... He's in good hands but he's only twenty-one... I'm too anxious to drive... What can I do? ... He'll be okay. I don't even remember if I prayed.

My mind was a plethora of mixed thoughts and emotions. I should call my husband Michael to help me with insight and direction. After filling him in on what I was told, Michael suggested that I contact

Maddy, my former mother-in-law and family matriarch. She would certainly be in the know on the whole situation.

According to Grandma Maddy, her son and my former husband David had been rushed to the hospital because he was having seizures. Matthew had driven their vehicle behind the ambulance. Evidently this was a common occurrence of the past and David would be seen by the doctor and then would go home by day's end.

Well, on this specific day, things were different. Matthew was having sharp chest pains and needed to be examined as well. The doctor then had my son rushed by ambulance to another more specialized hospital. This was serious and Grandma Maddy assured me that my boy was in the best hands and that there was nothing to worry about. I deemed her words to be calming.

Knowing that there was certainly nothing I could do on my end and feeling that I would probably be seeing Matthew AFTER surgery because I clearly couldn't drive in my current mental state, I chose to occupy my mind by continuing to work. My husband would help me get to New York safely. Despite everything, I did try to call Matthew anyway. To my surprise, he answered his cell phone, but it was as if nothing special was happening when he replied "Hi, mom, what's up?" Personally, I thought "Are you serious?" I surmised that he was trying not to worry me, that he was protecting me. Typical Matthew! He was always putting the feelings of others before his own. As he started ow, owing on the phone, forgive me Lord that I was taken back in time. I was reminded of an incident years ago when David was suffering with intense pain. It was a life-threatening situation and as I looked back, what stood out was fear.

A fleeting thought crossed the back of my mind. Was this truly all taking place or was it some sort of drama unfolding before me? Here was my Matthew, a young man going through trauma. I reassured my son, letting him know that he was in good hands, that the doctors would take good care of him, and just to relax. He said that he had to go because he was very tired, and we exchanged our goodbyes closing with "I love you."

The Lord had to have been completely in control because I do not have any clue as to how I could have finished my workday. He was definitely my "auto-pilot" with my brain and body working automatically to do what I had to do and what was expected of me. Thank You Lord for being behind the wheel.

Blurred moments are caught up in a flash of time....

My husband was not at all thrilled about the way everything went down. Here I was, the mother of an ailing son, I'm at work so naturally I'm going to be too upset to drive and then there's my daughter and son-in-law already on route to New York when I finally get the news and I probably could have ridden with them. After all, I am Matt's mother. I can understand Mike's irritation with all the unfairness and at the same time I also understand that everyone is in their own little world. Besides, with that side of the family, I've always been last for any important information and sometimes I was just plain kept in the dark. Truth is truth, forgive me if I sound bitter.

We tried calling to find out what hospital Matt was in, the first facility we called claimed he wasn't there, family members were not answering their phones, a completely frustrating situation. Again, I'm only Matt's mother.

Once we finally received a response, I put together two days' worth of clothing, knowing that I would be sleeping over at Grandma Maddy's house. Over the years, Maddy and I had always had a mutual respect and adoration for one another, so my being welcome there was a silent given. Consequently, Michael would stay home to avoid any awkwardness with my former in-laws. Everything was a go and I was now ready for the long drive.

I encountered sporadic traffic during the ride, but I remained in a peaceful state of mind anyway, listening to Christian music and thinking of Matthew with silent prayer. Everything was going to be okay.

Upon arriving at the hospital, I felt at a loss for direction. The first and only parking lot was entirely for handicapped parking. Off to the opposite side was one road and another separate road leading underground. More confusion. In the moment, the art of frustration closed in on me. Where do I park so I can just get inside and see my boy? My thoughts were scattered until they became jolted into awareness by the sound of my cell phone ringing. It was Sean wondering where I was. He directed me on a path that led me onto an incline road where I spotted Debbie at a crosswalk. Deb was my former sister-in-law, so I flagged her down. She got into my car and guided me to the correct parking garage.

Once parked, we met outside the back of my car. I inquired about Matt and her only response was shaking her head back and forth. "What do you mean?" I asked. A second time she shook her head, motioning no. I didn't question anything more. I just collapsed against Deb and moaned, sobbing loudly. My heart was breaking into a million pieces at this very moment. Falling against her, I cried hysterically. Not my son... Matthew!

I felt distraught and thrown into a bottomless pit, my mind pooling with darkness. NOOO! Is this a dream? It can't be real. What's happening? Plunge me into this sub-surreal climate of mourning. It's raw, it's real, and it hurts. Somebody wake me up from this nightmare. I'm going numb. I vaguely recall Deb inserting the words "I felt the same way." This is my child, it must be wrong, someone's playing a cruel joke, assorted questions racing through my brain. Bring him back!

I have never felt so brokenhearted and yet at the same time so in tune to my emotions as right at this very moment. I am forced to surrender myself here and now. The Lord most assuredly had to be guiding my steps because I don't know how I could have had the strength to face Tiffany with this shocking loss that we were all sharing.

No thank you but together we are on an ocean of grieving with no land in sight.

Please sort out what is wreaking havoc in my brain. I don't want to think, and I certainly do not want to suffer this horrific tragedy. I've been injected with an overdose of sorrow straight up and on another spectrum, I'm like a lonely hot bird searching for that one drop of water, trying to muddle through my existence.

Tiffany and Sean were sitting on benches outside of the hospital. I hugged my daughter and cried, my mind scurrying from reality. How could this be? What do I do now?

Snap shut alert: I want to see Matthew, I'm his mom and no one is going to stop me from seeing my boy. Sean brought me up to the emergency room. I recall a doctor saying something to the effect of being sorry. I was so numb that I passed that comment off with the words "that's okay" naturally rolling off my tongue. Really, that's okay? No, it's not okay!

My beautiful son lay there on the hospital bed appearing as if he were sleeping. He looked so peaceful. I ran my fingers over his spikey hair and kissed his forehead and his cheeks. I told him I loved him over and over. Without even thinking, I was uttering words of endearment, "I love you, Matt", "I love you, Matt", "I love you, Lord", freely flowing from my lips.

After a while Deb was standing across from me on the other side of the hospital bed and Sean was by my side. He asked me if I wanted to pray. Yes, of course…

"Our Father, which art in heaven,
Hallowed be thy name.
Thy kingdom come,
Thy will be done
In earth as it is in heaven.
Give us this day our daily bread.
And forgive us our debts,
As we forgive our debtors.
And lead us not into temptation,

But deliver us from evil.
For thine is the kingdom and the power and the glory forever.
Amen." (Matthew 6:9-13)

I thank God for Sean leading me in prayer and for knowing my heart enough to realize exactly what I needed at that moment. As we left the room, I went back to kiss Matthew one last time. It was as if I didn't want to leave his side yet knowing that it was inevitable that I depart.

Once I returned to the presence of Tiffany's company, I sat with her for a few minutes before calling Michael. My husband would have driven out to me, but we decided it was best for him to drive out in the morning. I then called a couple of friends from church, Debra and John and gave them the sad news about Matthew. Deb had formed an adoration for my son and was devastated. They offered to give Mike a ride out here to be with me. Thanking them both for their kindness, I informed Deb that my husband would be joining me in the morning.

Upon leaving the hospital, I rode with my daughter and her husband while my former sister-in-law offered to drive my vehicle back to Grandma Maddy's house. During the car ride, Pastor Jack called me. I was somewhat numb as he provided me with comforting words. Tiffany was in the front seat complaining that this was family time, that I shouldn't be on the phone. I brushed her concerns aside for the time being because this was something that I needed. I had just lost my son and I was devastated. I needed spiritual encouragement, something which Tiffany couldn't offer me at this time. Shortly thereafter, Pastor Lane called me. I didn't really know him very well and he was soon to be our new pastor, so I was a little on the reserved side with him. All in all, I appreciated both of my pastors for their consideration in reaching out to me and throwing me a lifeline so to speak. The Lord was sending me comfort before I even had a chance to realize what was happening.

As we gathered together in a heap on top of Grandma Maddy's huge bed, I hugged her and cried. Without thinking, the words came out "I lost two babies." My mind was connecting and expressing thoughts fluently while the pain in my heart was on overdrive. You see, I had lost a five- month old baby girl at the age of seventeen and hadn't thought about it in years. Yet here it was, zooming to the surface and I was now sobbing for both. The atmosphere was so somber and sad. We were all in total shock, every one of us, a massive state of disbelief.

Once I settled into the bedroom I would be using, I called Mom. I don't even recall what the hour was, I just remember inquiring if she was sitting down. Then I spoke the dreaded words "Matthew died." After a bit of silence, Mom asked if there was a car accident. I explained that it was something to do with his heart and that she needed to spread the word. UGH!

Tiffany and Sean were sharing a room down the hallway. People were situated in different areas, and there were five bedrooms altogether. As I drifted off, crying myself to sleep, I thought I heard Matt's voice say "Mom, I'm okay." I'm quite sure it was in my imagination with a lot of wishful thinking. Sometime, in the middle of the night I woke up, became aware of my surroundings and why I was there, then proceeded to cry again. My daughter came in and consoled me. I was thankful for her courage in that moment. The cycle of tears and sleep intertwined throughout the evening. It was by far the worst night of my life.

Considering the breaking dawn, I got up early and showered. I might as well have been a human puppet because I was undoubtedly just going through the motions. Dry my hair, okay... presentable, I guess. What then startled me was when I saw my eyes in the mirror. I never in my life knew what one's eyes looked like after an entire night of sobbing. They were so puffed up and red. I still refuse to believe that any of this is happening.

My husband had sent me a good morning text message, telling me that he was on his way. Michael called me as soon as he arrived into New York and I met him in a familiar shopping area. He encouraged me to get a bite to eat, however food was the last thing I wanted. I needed my husband's strength to help me through this turmoil. Many years ago, Michael had lost a wife tragically to a car accident, so he knew about sudden and unexpected loss, especially that of someone near and close to your heart. I was trusting and leaning on him to push me forward. He had persevered with his own tragedy over fourteen years ago and now he had the compassion to support me in my brokenness.

Since there were several twists and turns through town, Mike followed me to Grandma Maddy's abode. The house was in a nice neighborhood with a lot of beautifully manicured lawns. I just didn't know the names of the streets to get us there. The destination had a big arch shaped driveway so there was plenty of parking space. We were greeted at the door by David, my ex, and Joe, Maddy's companion. All of us congregated around the kitchen table for coffee and small talk. It was a pleasure to see courteous communication between my ex and my present spouse.

I truly had no interest in eating breakfast, but my husband urged me to have something. I forced down a little bit of scrambled eggs and an English muffin. Automatic pilot consumption in a mindless action of necessity. It was like remnants of a crazy dream unfolding before us all with the very cruel reality that we would never be seeing Matthew again, this was our new life. Well I don't like it.

...A block of time erodes into oblivion...

When the idea of food came to mind, I desired a thick corned beef sandwich on rye bread from a local deli, so Mike and I went for a ride. Upon reaching our place of interest, I didn't remember where along the strip mall building that this restaurant was located. I started to peek inside a pizzeria and when I stepped back out onto the sidewalk, a stranger began speaking to me. He was a casually dressed elderly gentleman, sporting a beard and he had been pulling a cart with grocery bags. "That's good food in there." I responded by saying "That's great but I'm looking for Winthrop Deli. Do you know where it is?" He pointed it out and I said, "Thank you." His reply ... "God Bless" ... My words... "God Bless you as well" and I proceeded to walk away. Out of the blue this soft- spoken man pronounced the word "hospital." I quickly spun around and stared at him in awe. Were my puffy eyes giving me away? To myself, I was pondering why he would possibly have said that of all things. He then made a statement and in shock I uttered "What?" The words that came out of his mouth next, I will remember for the rest of my life. His words and I quote, "It was a heart aneurysm, God told me to tell you", hand over his chest and pointing a finger at me. Michael wanted to make sure that this guy was for real, so he asked, "Oh, you believe in God?" and the man replied "Yes I do, and God told me to tell you" again pointing at me. I was totally dumbfounded. This was insane! God Himself was speaking to me and I'm only a small, simple person. It's true and God in all of His Glory was letting me know in my darkest hour that this stranger was His vessel and that God was using him as an angel. This one ordinary man, one who could easily blend in with the crowd, was serving God's purpose and in this isolated incident, it was in the form of a very special gift. I found comfort from his words and was completely amazed by this entire scenario. I had never heard of anyone else experiencing this, yet here it was in plain view for us at this very location here on earth. My Matthew must be with the Lord for sure! What mother wouldn't want to believe this after losing a child?

I ate that corned beef sandwich with a new relish for life stirring up inside of me. Mike and I replayed that whole scene filled with wonder by the entire abnormality of events. More so, we were awestruck with God, how He took this one person crossing my path and used him to relay such an important message to me. My Creator was giving me hope and I became very mindful that from this moment forward, my life was never going to be the same and that my faith in Him was taking a giant leap forward.

Lori, our friend from church had tried contacting me a couple of times. When I returned the call, she asked me if everything was all right, thinking it odd that she had accidentally called my number not once but twice. I filled her in on all the details from yesterday and then I shared my witness of God's angel today. She was astounded and rightfully so. This wasn't your common every- day occurrence transpiring during tragedy followed by such an unlikely phenomenon. What started out as black and white was unraveling into colors and the Lord definitely had my attention. Lori had some concerns pertaining to her family and we agreed to lift each other up in prayer.

Prior to Matt's passing, Mike and I had taken a mini vacation to Texas. While there I had picked up a baseball cap with the words "Don't mess with Texas" on it as a souvenir for Matthew. My heart and mind were prodding me to give the cap to Jason, Matt's best friend and side kick. My car felt guided as I made my way down Jason's road. The sight up ahead floored me. There in the distance were an array of cars on both sides of the street with writing on several of the back windshields. I saw the letters "RIP" and "Brother" with assorted personal messages added to that. A cluster of young people were gathered together while some were sitting on a wall. I knew that I had to stop. As if in a trance, I walked slowly towards the crowd. With my voice cracking and my eyes tearing up, I stated "You all loved my son?"

One by one they started coming over, hugging me and telling me how sorry they were for my loss. Some even proceeded to share with me how much Matthew had touched and changed their lives for the better. I was proud to hear all of this about my boy and it gave me a deeper understanding as to how many friends he really had. Oftentimes I would call him in the past and Matt would say "Mom, I'm with my friends." Okay, now I get it and being around his companions like this inwardly I concurred that they needed me as much as I needed them. Tenderly, I felt my son's loving spirit encircling each and every one of us. Being here in the center of his friends, I felt the presence of my boy's arms around me, hugging his momma. A feeling of peace lingered in the air.

There were four large poster boards taped around a tree near the road. The kids had signed all sorts of sentiments to Matthew. I wrote loving words to my son. It still seems so impossible! They had decorated Matt's car with flowers and candles along with personal items. There was a group photo taken of all of us standing in front of it.

Jason was very moved when I gave him the cap intended for my son. I explained to him that Matt would want him to have it and that I had a personal request. I asked him to please "put some miles on it," meaning to wear it to different places. He promised he would and wore it gladly.

This reminded me of how much Matt loved to travel. He had once taken a vacation to Maine with Mike and me. Oh, how he loved the alpacas! He enjoyed beach time and climbing rocks as well, but he was in his glory when he got to be "captain" of a small motorboat. Matthew loved the outdoors and he was always happy for us whenever we went on trips. There was one time we had a trip planned to tour Israel in 2012 and Matt had said "Oh, you're going to the Holy Land, you're going to where Jesus was." He knew of Jesus!

Seated at the kitchen table over at Maddy's, I spoke surface talk with David, just reminiscing about Matthew when he was younger. The hospital called asking for Matt's organs. I handed the phone over to my ex-husband, putting up my hands and not wanting any part of that conversation now or ever. David screamed at them "you're not cutting up my son" and told them to leave him alone. I wondered where Mike was, so I dialed his number. He had gone for a walk down to the docks at the end of the street, so I headed out to meet him. As I sauntered up the road at a casual pace, I heard Matt's voice very clearly say to me "Mom, I'm home now." This was completely unbelievable because in my way of thinking, the first place I thought of was Heaven! Perhaps I really DID hear my son's voice last night, telling me that he was okay, and if that is true, Thank You Lord for making this possible.

I shared this latest revelation with my spouse. I could appreciate Michael's concern for my welfare and because of his compassion and love for me, he was being overly protective, however the Lord already had His hand on me, and I was being pushed ahead steadily.

Later that night, in the company of my husband, I fell into a more restful sleep, until I was awakened by the sounds of Tiffany sobbing in the room down the hallway. Without hesitation, I went to my daughter and spoke reassuring words as I held her. I then pressed on to tell her about the angel, letting her know without a shadow of a doubt that her brother was truly in Heaven. She drew peace from me and became more tranquil. I felt an inner strength in comforting my girl.

The following morning, Mike and I sat in the kitchen with some of the other family members discussing funeral arrangements. With David's family being Jewish, I didn't know what would be decided. However, what I did know was that I did not want my son buried in a mausoleum. Matthew had accepted Jesus and wore a cross necklace. He had gone to church with me whenever he visited Connecticut and Matt had also attended church a few times with his New York friends. I certainly did not want him to be encased by cement inside a building, no offense against anyone. I just needed to know that my son's final resting place would be that of which was surrounded by nature such as trees, flowers, and the like.

As time marched forward, it didn't seem likely that any selections were being made to finalize the funeral plans so Michael and I mutually decided that he would head back home to take care of our responsibilities there and I would return later. Not having abundant monetary resources, I needed to see what was available for cash advances on my credit cards so that I could donate funds toward my son's burial expenses. In preparation of my homeward return, I left my cell phone in the back bedroom, letting it acquire a full battery charge.

I socialized in the dining area with Tiffany, David, and Inez, the housekeeper. I loved this beautiful Spanish lady who also had a heart for Christ. We had built a dear friendship over the years and she had known of all my concerns and worries for Matthew as well as how much I loved and missed him. Between us all, we were exchanging fun stories about our boy and it was even mentioned how a few years back Matt had helped his former boss by restoring the damage at the gentleman's business after a major flood. This made me proud to realize the extent of my son's care for others.

Eventually, it was time for me to head home. There were some things there that needed my attention. Prior to collecting my belongings from the bedroom, I noticed that I had a phone message. As I was walking back down the hallway, I heard Michael's voice telling me that he was so sorry to hear about my grandmother. What? Not again... Am I in an endless nightmare? My grandmother was in the hospital for hip surgery and I had known that she had come out of it fine. I fell to pieces, crying loudly and crumpling on the bench in the family room. Before I knew it, I was wailing. Inez and Tiffany came right over to me, holding my hand and my face, trying to calm me. Even Grandma Maddy who usually stays upstairs made her way down. My heart was broken yet again. My favorite grandmother, the one I could tell anything to and lean on besides my husband, was gone, too. This is too much. I feel like I'm drowning in sorrow.

Over time, an unknown calmness settled in. I can't really say that I had come to an acceptance with everything that had transpired. Honestly, I couldn't handle any more heartache. Somehow or other I was moving forward so I wasn't about to worry myself, trying to figure it all out. However, I can confirm that I was leaning on God, that He was making a way for me and I was mindlessly along for the ride.

... More socializing in the living room and a quick bite to eat...

Being captivated in the stillness of sorrow yet led in the calm of His peace, I proceeded with preparations to attempt the long trek home. It was around 5pm and I was estimating a minimum of three hours at least from here to there. My attention was partially dormant as I viewed cars up ahead weaving in and out without reason. And then it happened... third day in a row. Matt's voice broke into my aimless thoughts. He said "Mom, look for me." I pondered… hmm okay… the sky… the billboard… what or where. Within less than five minutes as I went over a crest in the highway, a seagull flew across in front of me at EYE LEVEL. Seagulls don't do that. Now I know in my faith that Matthew is certainly not a seagull but what I did realize is that this was a gift from God. To me, this was additional confirmation that Matt truly is okay. In many ways I was being covered with the Lord's presence which became abundantly clear when I started singing out "I Love You Lord, I Worship You, You Are My God…" The words and tune were flowing naturally from my lips. Smack-dab in the middle of my pain, my heart was singing "Savior King".[1] There is no explanation on how I could possibly discern and process my pain like this without the Lord directing my path. Jesus was surely behind the wheel as my autopilot yet again because I don't recall having any concentration whatsoever during the trip. Every so often, I would get caught up in traffic and when I was approximately an hour away, I contacted my sister Tami. I asked her if she could get our immediate family together over to Mom's house and I also filled in Mike about this plan as well. It was my desire to have everyone in one household where I would see them all for the first time in the wake of our loss. The love and support from my family was much needed, we each had just lost two people within two days.

With a steady calm, I entered Mom's house and met everyone in the sitting area. Clinging to my angel experience as comfort, I hugged and cried with Mom, Dad, Tami, my brother Allen, and my husband. These past few days had been unimaginable. Needless to say, I was emotionally exhausted by this point, so without delay, I completed the trek home with my hubby following directly behind.

It was good to lay in the relaxation of my own bed. I fell into a deep sleep until I was awakened for another bout of crying. I am aware that the road ahead of me is going to be long and then I recalled that a fellow sister in Christ had extended me an offer to reach out to her at any time, no matter the hour. I did utilize that offer several times to help pull me forward. Thank you, Rebecca.

Thursday morning found me to be a little more rested. Truthfully, I wanted to view these past few days as some sort of crazy nightmare, an April Fool's joke if you may, just to have Matthew jump out and say "Gotcha." But unfortunately, that wasn't to be. I told Michael that I wanted to see my dear friend, Sellie. She had always been like another mom to me and I thoroughly enjoyed her company. My call to her was received with a welcoming response. She and her husband Paul currently were entertaining family and friends but there was still room for me, so I headed there promptly. With a feeling of security and the Lord's encouragement, I spoke of my remarkable events along with my hurting heart. It was all positively overwhelming. Once I was able to put my mind at ease, I posed a question to Sellie and her friend asking them if they could help me with a collage. The answer was a favorable yes. You see, for myself, I was projecting ahead, devising a plan to celebrate my son's life at our church. It was my wish to share Matt's loving heart with others, and ideally putting together some special pictures would capture a portion of that desire perfectly. I thank You Lord for this sacred circle of kindness and love in the midst of very dear people.

Filled with complete oblivion, Jesus regulated my course once again as my car drove straight into the church parking lot. I walked into the front door and went directly to the altar. It was at that place that I let everything go, no holds barred. I cried, screamed, and wailed. My broken heart needed exposure and release. This was my moment, just between God and me, baring every possible raw emotion in my existence. This alone time with the Lord was highly necessary before I could even grasp the idea of facing any of my church family. I wasn't ready for that. I needed this opportunity to be able to handle my own new reality. I didn't like it but there wasn't any one thing that I could possibly do to change it. Surely, I could not be angry with God, after all He Himself blessed me with an angel, so without wavering, I must put my trust in Him.

It was strange how I exercised my faith but at times I have to confess that I was on and off the fence. I'm just being honest here, after these previous days with everything that came to pass, how could I not trust and believe in the Lord? I was being carried and there was no denying that fact. People were praying for my family as well as myself and I will never know who they all are, but their prayers of unity were most certainly being answered. My steps were being guided and I was merely a loose vessel being tossed side to side but in a forward direction. Unbeknownst to me, the Lord's plan was slowly emerging.

(Let me delve into the day ahead of me)

I took care of some financial affairs and then called Tiffany. It was necessary for me to have information on when the final services would take place. At first it appeared that the burial would be on Saturday, then the arrangements kept changing. Matt's friends wanted a service prior to the funeral, and they were upset. I could relate to their feelings. They wanted an opportunity to be able to say goodbye to their pal and they wouldn't have had that chance at a cemetery. Finally, I dialed my daughter's number again and received a snippy answer "We're eating." I was at the mercy of the power of frustration. All in all, the plans changed three times and the service would begin tonight. Being Matt's mom, I certainly had a right to be informed of this information sooner, however now it was abundantly clear that I would not be able to attend this evening's service. The drive was too long with traffic at this hour. As a result, I missed out on Matthew's companions expressing their love through stories and memories from what I was told.

With the dawn of Friday morning, Mike and I were on the road early. We brought nice garments with us and wore casual attire for the ride. The drive to New York was somber and nonchalant. My life has taken a new detour and things will never be the same. I'm a mom who lost a son, that's my title. I feel ill.

As soon as we arrived in New York, we headed to Jason's house. The kids (Matt's friends) presented me with photos and paraphernalia in which they had written loving notes on to say goodbye. After changing our wardrobe at Jason's, Mike and I met the others over at

Grandma Maddy's. It was now time for the limousine ride. I'm glad that my husband could stay with me as we rode with David, Tiffany, Sean, and the grandparents. Allen, Tami, and Mom met us at the funeral home. Many of Matt's acquaintances along with their parents were extremely kind in extending condolences toward myself and my family from Connecticut. So many caring people were pouring out their love upon us.

Shortly after entering the building, the family was shuffled off into a conference room. Once we all filed in, the Rabbi started asking questions about Matt, in a sense to get to know our loved one better. A few things were mentioned by others. Mike spoke up and related how Matthew had vacationed with us in Maine. Someone tried to shush him but we just ignored the action. Matt was part of our lives too. Eventually, the family was brought into another room with couches, perhaps a waiting area. Some family members were given black ribbons which they tore in unison, symbolizing an observance of mourning.

With an air of guardedness, I eased into "that room" with my son lying unseen in a wooden casket, feeling an indescribable void from within. It was a common denominator that every single one of us was missing Matthew, he was such a happy kid. There were a couple of photos on display off to the side, one with both Tiffany and Matthew and the other one of Matthew alone. Yes, a photo… This is what we had left of him, our photos and our memories. Outside of that was the brutally honest fact that Matt was currently separated from us. My daughter had written something very moving and special to share about her brother. His aunt Debbie and cousin Jason spoke nice words as well. I went up and recited The Lord's Prayer (Matthew 6:9–13) upon Joe's request but I was more than honored to do it. Filled with anguish, I was going with the flow. Lastly, Grandma Maddy stated that she had something to say. Her words… "I hate the devil for taking my grandson." These words hung in the air.

As the casket was being wheeled away, the crowd all fell in behind. Distraught, David leaned on it and sobbed. The immediate family assembled back into the limousine. Vehicles were proportionately in place for the funeral procession. The solemn ride to the cemetery began. During our cavalcade, stray automobiles tried cutting into our travel path. I witnessed a yellow hummer from our group zooming forward and stopping these intruders in their tracks. It was extremely surreal. Enough said.

At the site, the family had certain positions to stand in. It was very unusual and unfamiliar to me. The words of the service that followed became just a blur. This reality check was NOT registering. As the activities ended, everyone started walking out towards the roadway where the vehicles were lined up. I took notice when Matt's buddies lifted the hoods of their cars and in unison, they all began to rev their engines. The tears quickly sprang from my eyes without hesitation. This was such a beautiful act of love and respect on their parts honoring Matthew in this way. It was an endearing and memorable moment.

A reception was being held afterwards at the home of Matt's grandmother. There were assorted sandwiches, salads, and desserts. I had reached out to David every now and then out of respect and rightfully so, this was our child who was now gone. During the afternoon, I tried to contact Pastor Jack. As I mentioned previously, I was mentally preparing for my son's memorial celebration. It was of great importance for me to celebrate his precious life with friends and family in Connecticut. Since the pastor's time was limited, (he was in the process of moving to North Carolina) we settled on the date of the event to be held on May 25th. For the most part, I wanted his leadership in this matter because Matthew had met him and heard a couple of his sermons. Along with that, it was essential that I have some state of normalcy in the church with my recent loss.

The kids had organized a benefit to raise money for the family to help with funeral expenses. These friends were endlessly thoughtful and their love for my son was so sincere. Some kids reached out to me, bewildered by my calmness with everything. I explained about the angel and God's words to me, knowing that our beautiful Matthew was indeed in Heaven. It seemed as if a few of his comrades were looking to me for an answer. Well, Jesus was that answer!!

Through God's love, our hearts were all being connected right now with our common affection for Matthew.

Emotionally depleted and extremely tired, Michael and I chose to call it a night. We had reserved a hotel room in a nearby town, knowing that Grandma Maddy's house was currently full.

Following a good night's sleep, I found a special surprise awaiting us the very next morning. Outside in the parking lot, there were cherry blossom petals coating my entire vehicle. Why cherry blossoms? you might ask. Well, there just so happens to be that same kind of tree growing near my son's resting place and I felt the connection. Thank You Lord for this gift and for opening my eyes enough to receive it.

Prior to our departure, we went to lunch at Winthrop Deli. A few of the kids joined us there. It felt natural to be here at this moment along with these special individuals. Stories were told and memories were passed around exposing our mutual love and respect for my boy. Being a mom, from the bottom of my heart I wanted every one of them to have good goals and productive lives. Matthew always knew that I would want the best for him and Tiffany and with that, he would wish the same for all of them. As we parted ways with sadness, there was also an air of inner joy. God's love.

On the return ride, I felt a spiritual nudge tugging at me to drive to the residence of two very dear friends. I wasn't prepared to go home yet, furthermore there was something that needed to be addressed. John and Debra welcomed us in, and it was sheer joy to spend time with fellow Christians. Mike and I were able to share our account of uncommon occurrences that played out as of recent, including the man who served as God's angel. The entire chain of events was intense and unheard of, but it was REAL. Finally, I spoke of the topic that was troubling me, my other reason for stopping at this location. I was feeling apprehensive about church tomorrow. It would be Mother's Day and I wasn't sure how I would handle that. Would people be all over me with my loss of Matthew? My fear was that I would be smothered even though I have an awesome and caring church family. Deb encouraged me to sit with her, that we

19

would arrive late once praise and worship had already begun. The lights in the sanctuary would be dimmer. Amazing how in my time of need, I was being shown a by-product of the Lord's love and grace. And to think that God was navigating my entire path while I was filled with so much grief that I couldn't possibly have been able to handle these conditions on my own. Nonetheless, here He was, leading me to the home of faithful friends, giving me an opportunity to express the depth of my sorrow. Who but Jesus could place me where I was meant to be, providing me with a comfortable way to attend church tomorrow? I went home feeling like I was in a bubble of temporary peace.

Good morning, world. Here it is, the day is upon us... Mother's Day. Never in a million years could I have pictured this holiday to be anything like this. A day full of tears but for what reason? I sit with feelings of anxiety and loneliness. My daughter is still in New York, because her dad is in the hospital. Even so, I am thankful to God that I have Michael by my side on this day that has always been special to me with my children. He is here to share the truth, my truth. I hurt... I feel loss... I feel emptiness... I miss Matt. But even though I feel all these things, I will not turn away from the Lord or turn my back on church. The Lord is my Rock, He is the One who will see me through, and I cannot do this without Him. But God, how I hurt!

Seated away from my usual place and next to our dear friends, we are in the house of the Lord. As the songs of praise wash over me, myself being covered with periods of numbness, I surrender to the tears that start rolling down my cheeks. This is my emotion, this is me right now, and I don't have any clue as to how long I am going to feel this way. There's a raw open wound deep in my heart which has completely crushed me. Lord, help me, my burden is heavy. Saturate this mother's broken spirit with Your healing and Your mercy, as I weep at Your feet. I sense hands laid upon me, lifting me in prayer, and I appreciate these vessels, Lord, these faithful people with compassionate hearts reaching out to help a sister in need. I know that we as a body of Christ are to be there for one another, however right now I'm only capable of moving forward one instant at a time. I am left to grasp at my beautiful memories of Matthew, but Lord, truthfully, it's too soon. I'm not there yet.

Throughout much of the sermon, I felt hollow and aloof with the constant reminder of Mother's Day echoing throughout my brain. I feel empty... empty-handed...empty-hearted...empty-spirited, although the Lord does keep nudging me to keep going.

Let me be honest here. Prior to the loss of my son, my faith really was lukewarm. I believed in Jesus Christ, but at the same time, I would also put Him away on the shelf. I would bounce back and forth between standing up for righteousness and on occasion, I would allow myself to be pushed around. I wasn't seriously making my stand for Christianity. But I do have to tell you, once I lost Matthew and then heard from God Himself, I knew that things would never be the same again. My faith was jumpstarted, skyrocketing it into full gear, full throttle if you may. My Savior was carrying me day by day, and moment by moment. He placed people in my path as well as life itself. The events that followed were countless and I will never truly know how many people, acquaintances and others who prayed for me personally as well as my family, forgive my repetition, I am thankful. Where there once was a lot of discord, I discovered peace, His peace that surpasses all understanding (Philippians 4:7) and healing, leading me to never look back. I am a child of God, here, now, and forever, and because of what Jesus did for me, what He did for all of us, I get to see my son again one day. I get to thank Jesus Himself for dying on the cross for our sins to give us eternal life. Neither crisis nor turmoil, nothing that we would ever experience could compare to the pain and suffering that our Lord had to endure. He is our Light in the darkness.

Consequently, in the peace and the stillness of our home, there was no likelihood of any activities following our return from church. My mind was weightless so I would never expect the unexpected, but lo and behold, that's exactly what came into being. I received a unique gift. It came in the form of a simple knock at the door. Upon opening it, there stood Anne, a lovely woman who happens to be

Tiffany's mother-in-law. In her hands were a dozen beautiful purple and white roses. As she wished me a happy Mother's Day, she further explained how an angel kept whispering in her ear "Please get my mom some flowers and make sure they're purple." My favorite color! I immediately started crying and thanked her for making my day extra-special. My son was blessing me through Anne's actions and the Lord is the one who made all this possible. Do you believe in miracles? I know that I sure do.

As I dig deep, dive, and absorb dimensions of the past, I can reflect and flourish in my precious memories. My healing was advancing forward, but in every aspect, the progression was exceedingly slow. My God was pushing me bit by bit and at other times He was carrying me. As I rested in His assurance, it was evident that I was not alone. Sure, I had my husband, as well as my family and friends reaching out in phone calls and in prayer which I appreciated, but in all truthfulness, they couldn't be available at every split second daily. Thank God that we all have a god who is omnipresent and with us at ALL times.

I felt a sudden need to visit Justin's mom to wish her a holiday greeting before the day ended. Lisa was very welcoming with open arms. Our sons had been best friends in earlier years when Matthew had lived with me. I used to reside less than five minutes from her, and our boys would ride their bikes to each other's houses. They were inseparable. She had heard of Matt's passing as did Justin. I shared my angel story with them, and they were quite amazed. Justin offered his services to help me in any way possible, so I suggested that perhaps he could mow our lawn because my husband's schedule was limited, and this would be a wonderful surprise for him. I appreciated their kindness and felt a sense of serenity in their company. It was so great to see them, especially since so much time had elapsed since our last visit, and besides that, Matthew was dear to all of us. On another note, I was proud of the young man Justin turned out to be. He was a hard worker as well as a college student and he was making something special of his life. I was extremely happy for him.

I was overjoyed when Tiffany called to wish me Happy Mother's Day. I feared that she had forgotten, being with her dad and all. In the end, I was blessed with hearing from both of my children, in a sense. My day had satisfaction written all over it.

Monday, May 13th

Here we go, one week later, and today we are burying my grandmother. It will only be a small intimate ceremony at the gravesite. Michael and I stopped at a grocery store nearby to purchase some flowers. I picked out a small pretty bouquet which I found to be favorable. At the cemetery, a lot of hugs were circulated among the relatives, however deep down a part of me was still quite numb. Grandmama, as I affectionately called her, would be buried near Grandpa and Uncle John. As a matter of fact, my firstborn was buried on these very same grounds in the baby section. Allow me to be swayed into emotional sedation. I was pleasantly surprised to see my cousin Diane attending, she was from my dad's side of the family. This was my mom's mother who had passed. While we all watched, my Gram's ashes were placed into the plot as the preacher spoke. Half-listening and half-comatose, I became more attentive to the conversation when I heard the grandchildren recapping special memories of their own about Gram. Laughter was in abundance. I had given a few of my flowers away but explicitly hung onto two of them. I placed both blossoms into the hole, one for Grandmama and one for Matt. Next, I revealed my favorite memory of how I would call up Gram and tell her that I knew she was having a party, so it was time for all her men to leave. She lived alone and she would laugh at my teasing.

My Gram... she made me feel complete and whole. She filled a void in my life when I was feeling indifferent toward my parents. She possessed kindness, love, and understanding of family life. My

Gram was also very witty and sharp. Alertness at the age of ninety-two, I not only loved her but had a deep admiration for her. Simply said, I could be an adult or childlike in her company. The warmth of my heart was being tested for sure. Herein lies a choice before me... become bitter or love deeper... my son AND my grandmother... I chose LOVE!!

Still it was hard to accept that they were both gone. How could I even begin to embrace the fact that I had lost two very dear people in my life in a matter of two days? Yet at the same time, in my faith, how could I not believe that they were indeed in Heaven together? And with that in mind, I had hope and assurance that I would be seeing them again one day in paradise. I'm completely immersed with the reality of death, but I do believe that one day we will live with Jesus and there will be no more tears or sorrow or even death. (Revelation 21:4) Praise God!!

A small reception congregated at Aunt Pat's place after the service. I loved being in the company of my cousins, chatting incessantly. While there, I also informed them about the date that was scheduled for Matthew's Celebration of Life. Photos were passed around as more tales were being told. Considering all that had transpired, it was a light atmosphere. Feeling fatigued, Mike and I parted ways but with the anticipation of visitors, knowing that Diane and Allen would be stopping by our house shortly thereafter.

Oh, what a blessing to be in the presence of my brother and my cousin. As we reminded ourselves of certain interactions with Matt, we were all rolling with laughter. What joy, my heart was leaping! Ahh, the medicine of laughter. The stress and anxiety were just melting away. This was highly essential for one and all.

As if that weren't enough, we were blessed yet again. Sue, my dear friend from church, had arranged for suppers to be delivered every evening this week and tonight Mike and I were receiving the very first meal which included a thoughtful sympathy card with comforting words. We were being showered with grace. I honestly felt like we were in the center of a circle with loving people in unison surrounding us, holding hands, and praying for us. God had us under His Fold, of this I am convinced.

Hello Tuesday morning, this is my first day alone. I'm alive, I'm breathing, and my emotions are paralyzed. Empty space in my head, white noise. Serene, quiet, holding tight to my angel story, and living with a gaping hole in my heart. I'm truly struggling here because this is the hardest thing that I have ever had to deal with ever. It doesn't seem fair but who am I? The Lord continues to slide me forward. I'm not looking for sympathy here, I'm only trying to survive. This leads me to believe even more so that God is lifting me up since I have no desire to hit the bottle or cloud my brain with drugs. I'm facing grief straight up and it's not pretty. Let HIS SON shine in.

It was a pleasure to see Justin arrive at our house with his own lawnmower. My husband deserved to have something nice awaiting him later after a hectic workday. This duty of yardwork was long overdue. Engulfed in a spirit of gratitude, I reminisced about Matt and Justin years ago, two young boys spray painting their bikes. Looking back in reflection, I smiled. Leaving Justin to his task, I went to run an errand. A copy of Matthew's birth certificate was required in order to receive his death certificate. Unfortunately, this was not going to be a pleasant chore, but it was a necessary one. At any rate, I hadn't been on the highway for very long when I spotted a car that looked just like Matt's headed in the opposite direction.

Strange though it seemed, how in the heck could that be happening? That car looked exactly like my son's dark blue Celica. Am I dreaming or in some sort of time warp? Matt's coming to my house and this has all been a weird joke. Just get me off this next exit and return home. Home, back to reality and Matthew is NOT THERE. I've been played for a fool but that's not surprising for someone who's been riding on their own emotions. Time to motivate myself to move on and don't forget to breathe.

What an unbelievable sight that was! To my knowledge, my son's wheels were parked in front of Jason's abode. Once I composed my thoughts, I gave the boy a call. He acknowledged me as "Mom" which was very endearing to me. I'm sure you could imagine my astonishment and disbelief when I was told that yes, the car had been moved to someone's garage. Shocking! The timing, the circumstance, nothing could match it. The hands of God at work yet again! I am so thankful that He has given me eyes to see, alerting me to my surroundings along with these amazing miracle wonders.

Michael was extremely grateful for the freshly mown grass, besides being happy that it was one less thing for him to be concerned about. He was being very attentive towards me, making sure that I was okay. Surprisingly enough, as I was placing one foot in front of the other, it began to formulate within me that the Lord had my back so to speak, in fact He had all of me and I was being transported moment by moment. That's the only way I can describe it, so forgive me if I sound repetitive. It's the truth! He was indeed lifting my burdens as well. There wasn't anything that my husband could do to make my journey any easier other than to hold me when I was in tears. On other occasions I would either call my mom or my sister and cry with them over the phone. They were terrific and they understood the depth of this momma's pain.

By nightfall, I was starting to find solace in sleeping with a teddy bear in my arms. This wasn't your typical ordinary stuffed toy by any means. It held an unspoken bond because my son had handstitched this little guy with his own hands, stuffing and all. Many a tear was shed upon this dear possession and it helped me to feel closer to my boy. It was like my own personal connection, from my heart to Matt's.

From here on out, I concentrated on taking care of the closest tasks at hand. I couldn't handle anything more than that. As of recent, I was considering going back to work the following Monday until I decided that I wasn't emotionally ready. Matt's Celebration of Life was a little more than a week away and that immediately became my focal point. I wanted to show the best representation of who Matthew was as a person and just how special he was. Mainly, I wanted to share his love which all leads back to God because He loved us first. So, for now, work would just have to take a back seat since I honestly couldn't handle it at this present time. I had suffered a deep blow and was struggling to come back to the surface.

One day at a time, step by step, moment by moment, breath by breath, Lord, take my hand…

As I began to settle into the mundane activities of daily living, something occurred to me totally out of the ordinary. While reminiscing, it crossed my mind that I had witnessed a rainbow in the same location behind our house twice over the course of two weeks. Simply incredible! It was beautiful and when I think of a rainbow, I am reminded of God's promise to us, and how we will have eternal life through accepting Jesus as our Lord and Savior. Therein lies my hope.

I could never have envisioned that there would be such a beautiful array of miracle moments, and to think that they all began with an angel, a stranger that God used as His vessel which turned out to be such a significant gift for me. It altered my faith drastically.

Yes, I have the Lord in my heart, and He really is helping me through this pain but that's not to say that I'm on an easy ride by any means. It's still hard. I am human after all and when I take my eyes off of Jesus, that's when I feel sorry for myself. I am a mother who lost a child and not just one child but two. I used to think that I had gone through so much trauma in my lifetime that I had received my fair share and that would be enough. As a result, the rest of my life should be great. Well, hello! My life has undoubtedly taken an unexpected turn. I'm not happy as far as this matter is concerned however there's not any one thing that I can do to change it. I'm disappointed and discouraged, I miss Matt, and Tiffany is still with her father. I FEEL EMPTY AND FRUSTRATED!! It's not easy to lose a loved one. Sometimes I feel as if I'm standing in the shadows of my life, watching as activities go on around me, like nothing has changed. Well, everything has changed for me. Living in this daily realm of forced motivation, I inhale and I exhale. I am nonetheless still present, and I have made it through another day without my son. From here on out,

I realize that each and every day is going to be different, whether I cry a puddle or an ocean.

To be brutally honest, I teeter totter between grief and hope. Certainly, I want to be leaning more towards hope but grief sure keeps getting its evil grip on me. Still feeling raw in my sadness because my loss is so new, I'm told that my emotions are normal. I must accept the fact that I am on one walloping rollercoaster ride with my mixed emotions but thankfully I'm in the hands of God.

Okay, enough feeling sorry for myself. It's time to humble myself before the Lord in complete abandonment, casting my cares onto Him. I can't erase my situation so it's quite obvious that I will be grieving for a lengthy amount of time. Because of that, it's apparent that I'm unable to help anyone else with their feelings right now. With my husband by my side, and people praying for our family, I will get beyond this with the help of the Lord. Enough said, it's time to set my sights on Matthew's memorial service.

I was gifted with a beautiful bonsai tree from a high school classmate. Seeing this indoor plant, I was briefly brought back in time. My thoughts awarded me with a glimpse from the past, a memory of myself with my two children watching <u>The Karate Kid</u> together.[2] There was an essence of tranquility with the rekindling of this precious memory, this calming touch from days gone by.

In the middle of a temporary lull in activity, I contacted Matt's companion Sam asking if I could get a copy of a certain video that another friend had created. It included a compilation of photos portraying my son with friends and family alike. The song *"Far Away"* by Nickelback played beautifully in the background.[3] With much compassion and understanding, she granted my request.

Allow me to delve into the storage unit searching for old portraits of Matthew or even current ones. There are so many totes to search through, it was quite overwhelming, but I must remember that I'm on a mission here. After much digging, I have come up with a few pictures of Matt, some with Tiffany and some without, all of which will be perfect for the collage. It goes without saying that I was ecstatic when I stumbled upon a unique gem, it was like discovering hidden treasure. I felt as if the Lord Himself had pointed it out to me and subconsciously I could picture my son saying "Mom, use this…" I won't disclose the identity of the item until the ceremony and for even more privacy, I am going to cover it in wrapping paper so that even my husband won't know what it is. Out of sight and out of mind. Bottom line, it's going to fit in wonderfully with my dedication to Matt.

I was being propelled ahead in a steady rhythm which was satisfying my eagerness to honor Matthew's remembrance. Now I know that I've mentioned this several times before about how important and how special this future event for my son was to me and it may all sound like a broken record to you, but truly I am not obsessed. I'm just a desperate mom who's trying to hang onto her son a little bit longer, and if this is how I accomplish that, so be it. I wanted to bring out the joy and beauty of his life, along with his impact on others and not dwell on the sadness and finality of a funeral. Personally, I believed that my boy's life was now in a different form, in a different place, one that we won't comprehend completely while living here on this earth. Only God has the authority to endorse favor upon our past, present, and future.

With that being said, my actions were not my own as the photos "floated" through my fingers. In all seriousness, my intention was to offer a loving tribute for my child. It was as if my hands were on autopilot perfectly placing each selection precisely and strategically into a beautiful and heartfelt masterpiece. The added sayings and words were a bonus. I just remember going with the flow so to speak, being pushed by the Spirit. Imagine this… the Lord already had Matthew's Celebration of Life lined up fittingly and I was along for the ride orchestrating His works through my actions.

> The splendor of a King, clothed in majesty
> Let all the Earth rejoice, all the Earth rejoice
> How great is our God, sing with me
> How great is our God, and all will see
> How great, how great is our God.[4]

Whisper Your Light and Your Peace into my life, O Lord.

Tami was truly a godsend since Matt's passing. Whenever I called my sister, she was there for me, listening to me crying and just loving on me through some very rough days. Without my knowledge, Tami had made a video capturing pictures of Tiff and Matt growing up while the tune *"Heaven Was Needing a Hero"* by Jo Dee Messina played in the background.[5] She had emailed me this on Mother's Day as a gift and I hadn't noticed it until several days later. Clearly, I was so preoccupied with sorrow, but like I mentioned before, my sister was a true godsend.

Wherever I go and whatever I do, I keep making my way forward in this method of survival. I'm all right for a little bit, then I begin to sink and as the Lord lifts me up, I'm okay for a while longer until I sink again. Just picture me as a floater who gets pressed underwater again and again and the cycle between good and evil continues. Or better yet, you can label me as a target that's been shot with an arrow straight through the heart. Grief sucks! It hurts and it can kill. I don't wish this pain on anyone. Being confident in knowing that Jesus is by my side allows me the ability to persevere. There will be battle scars and some wounds will war against healing but essentially this is just my earthly body. It is important that I value the many people both known and unknown that are praying for me to withstand this trial, this fight, and above all, this pain. As I linger in gratefulness, it amazes me how much God really loves us. My eyes can't identify anything presently, but He must have some mighty plans for my life and as I blindly remain persistent to the ongoing struggle, the Lord will show me joy. I'm not sure how but I will trust in Him anyway.

Speak into my heart, speak into my soul, and let me cling to You, Lord. Yes, I'm at a loss for words but You are bringing me into a new language, a new insight, and a new vision. Speak to me in a way that Your tears fall upon me like droplets of rain soaking into my being, into my very soul as You mourn beside me and with me. You understand the depths of my pain. Let me rise above that pain in the same way that the fog lifts after the rain.

Ahh, but to dream that Matt is here by my side, we're eating chips and dip and watching a cool movie together, the way things were and how they'll never be again.

Why does it have to be this way, along with that, why did I have to lose two of my three children? What is God's purpose for me and where is He taking me in this lifetime?

Up and down, wafting and drifting, I'm here and I'm not, in and out of conscious thoughts. Pinch me, these emotions are real. Stillness, grief, numbness, hope, pain, I miss Matt, at times walking inside a bubble, feeling but not feeling, just breathing, more hope, not using any substance to drown out the pain, slowly getting a little more sleep, I feel the Lord with me, He is my strength.

Enter Saturday...

Birthdays are usually so joyful, a day when one feels special and happy to be alive, an observance where one is recognized with adoration. Well, today is mine and I don't feel joy. My movements are mechanical and I'm trying to look up but it hurts to lift my head. Lord, lift my chin, please help me. I'm a mom who lost a child and life itself just isn't pretty right now. In this pool of sorrow like quicksand, I'm sinking deeper and deeper.

Be still my soul, the Lord is with me...

In retrospect, I ask the question "Why?" Despite everything, I have to bear in mind that our days are all numbered. The Lord blessed me with children, He alone has the power to give and take away. I had Matthew for twenty-one years, not all perfect ones but certainly forever special ones to me. He was the peacemaker who loved everybody so why wouldn't it be understandable that I would miss him so badly?

While I weep in the kitchen, I sense his face next to mine similar to the times when he would hug me from behind and wrap his arms around the front of me and our faces would be side by side. My son was so tall that my head could easily have been used as his chin rest. Despite my heartache, I am aware of Matt's presence wrapped around me. Sure, maybe one might think I'm crazy, but I truly believe that God is gifting me with this moment. Grant me the right to smile in reminiscence.

Okay... I can't fathom why a child could ever die before their parents although I'm not the keeper of my own universe. I'm not the Creator who knows all and sees all. My livelihood is along for the ride but it's not for my path, it's for the path He chose for me. I have made the choice to let the Lord lead my life. He has sight of my future and what I may envision as light could in fact be darkness. Our eyes are not as pure as His eyes and His ways. Dear Jesus, light up my path.

With that being said, I recall that the church is having a benefit yard sale for Feed the Need. This gives me an open opportunity to visit my church family, and at the same time, it allows me the freedom to readily leave at a moment's notice, no questions asked. I still have breath and I'm aiming to live as I take the hand of God.

Browsing and socializing at my own pace, my friend Debra has gifted me with a special angel. I feel vulnerable enough to share my authentic feelings with her. Tears on the stairs... symbolically at the bottom step where my journey was still beginning.

Without any sense of clarity, the day progressed forward as if in a blur and no offense intended toward any of my loved ones around me but my efforts to advance beyond this point were a true struggle. I'm trying my best to withstand this heartache.

Sundays were my day of resting in the Lord's presence, from listening to the sermon in the morning, although my concentration was downright difficult with an unsettled mind, to Sunday night prayer. One evening I found myself wailing uncontrollably, the hurt just kept pouring out of me as I expressed myself to Our Lord. It was then that I discovered what a wonderful prayer warrior and sister in Christ that I had in my friend Hazel. She had met my son and adored the polite young man that he was. I valued her friendship and as she lifted me spiritually in my desperate time of need, she cried alongside of me. Thank You God for placing her in my life as another lifeline.

Okay... I need to now shut off the independent part of my brain, also known as the selfish part. It's not all about me. Yes, I am hurting however it's time to focus on the future and what's straight ahead... the present... the here and now.

Focal point... Celebration of Life for Matthew... Full speed ahead.

- 11x14 canvas print of Matt
- 2 collages with easels for each side of altar
- New York décor with stuffed dogs and flowers
- video from New York honoring Matt's memory
- poster boards signed with love from Matt's New York friends
- flyers to pass out with order of ceremony
- guest book donated by a postal customer for people to sign in
- eulogy written out and wrapped surprise awaiting the right time
- 3 songs picked out for memorial service
- a dress to wear in Matt's favorite color – blue

I believe that I now have all things needed. Everything is in place.

Let the service begin.

Together under one roof in the house of God, all friends and family alike are here to embark on a journey. Through this special ceremony, we will show our respect for Matthew, agree upon our love for him, support one another in our loss, and lift up our shared memories of him, memories that all include LIFE. None of us know where our emotions will take us, expressed or not. We are all presently here with openness and God is in control.

Pastor Jack began the service with an opening prayer. He had met Matthew on previous occasions when my son was in town visiting.

Matt seemed to like the way the pastor preached and was spiritually touched by his sermons. At times, he would ask me questions for clearer understanding. During one such visit I can recall the entire congregation reciting the sinner's prayer, my son included. Right now, on this day, it was crucial for me to maintain a sense of familiarity.

> Amazing grace, how sweet the sound
> That saved a wretch like me
> I once was lost but now I'm found
> Was blind but now I see.

Let the chords fill this room, this sanctuary with words of humbleness and humility.

> T'was grace that taught my heart to fear,
> And grace my fears relieved;
> How precious did that grace appear
> The hour I first believed.[6]

Such a truly beloved hymn and the words are well known to so many. Personally, I feel like it's a song of the ages, a classic in its own way and as we shift gears for the next song, love fills the air. It doesn't matter to the Lord if you have a good voice or sing out of tune. As we praise Him, it's all music to His ears. Sing unto the Lord.

> And now the weak say I have strength
> By the spirit of power that raised Christ from the dead
> And now the poor stand and confess
> That my portion is You and I'm more than blessed.

> I love You Lord, I worship You
> Hope which was lost, now stands renewed
> I give my life to honor this
> The love of Christ, the Savior King.[7]

This song, this very song... I was singing the chorus on the highway on my way home two days after losing my dear son! How could this even be possible without having the Lord in my life? I was too preoccupied to notice how God had this entire service already planned. In fact, I didn't even know all the lyrics, only parts of the chorus, but on that day, merely two days after losing Matt, with my heart out on a sleeve... singing praises to Our Lord! Another small puzzle piece if you may that was fitting perfectly where it was meant to be.

Michael approached the podium and shared some scripture readings on love. He then went on to describe the impact Matthew had upon everyone, whether you met him for five minutes or five years, how your life was touched in such a positive manner. My husband had a good relationship with his stepson and I knew Mike's heart was hurting and that he was trying to be strong on my account. We were all trying to clamber our own way out, away from the dark clutches of death.

As we focused our attention on the wall screen, a video presentation came into view revealing a beautiful collection of photos featuring Matt with friends and family enjoying life. A very touching song was playing in the background. Tiffany and I hugged and cried together. Our Matthew was so full of life. I was extremely grateful that some of Matt's friends from New York were able to attend and also that they could witness this special celebration of my son's life.

It was now time for me to speak and I have to admit that I felt somewhat nervous. Wearing a long blue dress, I held a sense of regard towards my son knowing that this was his favorite color. A sudden inner strength emerged.

With the fervency of an expectant mother, my eulogy was waiting to be birthed. To God be the Glory!

Just like in the story of Moses where as long as his arms were raised high, the Israelites would prevail in battle, I knew that I was not alone on this stage with all of my vulnerabilities while I expressed a loving account of Matthew. I was in fact being held up from each side at my weakest moment, meaning this very moment right here and now. Here in front of all my friends and family, I was able to minister to what the Lord had already done in my life and was still doing. There was no turning back. This entire memorial was being anointed and I could feel it. Yes, I had sadness and tears but I also had hope. Hope in Our Father!

Here are the words I spoke...

Matthew Scott, my son, my sweet boy, boundless energy, lots of mischief, lots of fun, FULL OF LIFE!!

Matthew was born with a club foot and had surgery at a very young age. As a baby, he wore a cast which was later switched to special open toe shoes that could be hooked into a foot brace. He was a clever baby and these medical care items were not going to stop him from having great speed (Matt's motto: have arms and knees, will travel). Our family lived in a raised ranch, so with the concept of stairs, a gate was necessary for his doorway. Well, no obstacle for him. Throw a pillow on the opposite side, place something soft over the top of the gate, and then gather empty baby wipes (Chubs) containers made of hard plastic and stack them one on top of the other. The color sequence was unimportant. The end result: Matthew's escape with a soft landing.

I can recall a time when both Tiffany and Matthew had four-wheelers and would ride up and down the driveway. I would stress to them "Do not go past the telephone pole at the end of the driveway." For the most part, they were pretty good, occasionally zipping around the other side just to push my buttons. I did however find out in later years from a neighbor that they had been going on the main road, across the street, and down to the river when Mom wasn't home. Tiff often instigated the action and Matt always followed.

Over the years, Matthew and I visited back and forth between here and New York. He would come out for holidays and sometimes during summer vacation when he wasn't bowling. He loved to go to family outings (picnics, graduations, and birthdays). Previously, he went on a trip with Mike and I to Maine. My son loved the outdoors and all that it offered. He was always open to adventure. I missed him a lot but we kept in touch.

One morning last year we found a note stuck to the front door shortly after 4am. It read "It's 4:07am and I'm watching you, call (516) 419- ....". Recognizing that this was a New York area code written on this paper, I was hopeful that it was Matthew. I dialed the number, and my little brat answered, pretending to be sleepy and unaware of what I was talking about with the note, and afterwards pulling into my driveway. My son had also placed a second note on my car saying "I see you" in case I missed the first message. He knew our schedule of letting the cat out, getting ready for work for Michael, myself for the gym, and Matt had planned it out perfectly. His friend Jay was with him and despite the early hour, I was immensely pleased with this unexpected but happy surprise. Besides that, Matt gave the best hugs.

Matthew also enjoyed going to church with me. From chasing him around the pews when he was a little boy to attending Christmas Eve candlelight services in later years, and then more recently, reciting the sinner's prayer, Matt felt a peace in his life. He took some of the lessons with him and opened his heart to all.

I continued by expressing how Matthew loved both friends and family alike in New York and Connecticut. Through the Lord, I was being filled with such boldness as I continued to speak. My words were stated audibly and fluently as I familiarized them with the miraculous angel story about the stranger that God used for His purposes, His vessel that played a distinctive role in my life during my darkest hours. With the Lord by my side, I felt very secure. Otherwise, how could I have stood up here, a mom speaking about a child that she lost so unexpectedly? Nevertheless, the Lord had me, He had my back, He had my voice, in fact He had all of me. Here, these people were assembled together in this sanctuary to support myself and my family but instead my feeling was that I was giving them hope by showing them how the Lord was working through me.

Now that I clearly had their attention, it was time to reveal Matt's gift for them. I had wrapped it so that no one would see it and for some added suspense. This was a pleasant surprise for one and all, so here it is....

--- Matt's Only Diary---

I told everyone to be understanding, sympathetic, and to just be there supporting Matthew with his precious words that he wrote as a young child, words from his heart.

Okay, Matt, you wanted me to share this, so here goes…

Dear diary, yesterday Julie would not share with her marbles. I never liked her in my whole life and she never liked me. she is my enimie. I hate her so much. one day she said my friend is fat and I said she is not. Julie is very fat. my friend said she was a cow because she is so so fat. last year she was at my other baby siter. Julie ways 200 pounds because she is so fat. no one can pick her up. My friends name is Shana. She hates Julie too because she kept calling Julie fat. Julie's hair looks like a boy. first time I saw her she looked like a girl but when she got a hair cut she looked like a boy. Julie thinks I'm fat but she really is. She always writes about me but today I'm writing about her. Julie lies to my baby siter and I don't know why. she said that Shana was fat and I told Shana and Shana asked what did you say about me. Then Julie said that she did not say that.

The room filled with the blessed sound of laughter. Matthew was yet again filling people with joy, always wanting to make everyone happy.

My closing words were "Thank you for so many beautiful memories. I love you Matt always. Grandma is with you."

Tiffany got up and expressed her love for her brother with heartfelt words and unique recollections, mentioning how special the bond was between her and Matt. I knew how important this was to her as she spoke with deep sincerity and affection.

Jason, Matt's buddy, also known as his brother from another mother, relayed how this was too soon for a time such as this, how he should have been speaking at Matt's wedding or something more joyful. He explained how his friend had two families, one in New York and one in Connecticut and further disclosed how Matt could be childlike with his mom and was more of an adult with his dad.

I loved hearing him say how much Matt loved Tiffany and myself. Being his momma, these were endearing words to hear.

Finally, my friend Pat embellished on Matthew's younger years when she would stop by for Sunday morning breakfast and what a loving young boy Matt was.

Pastor Jack completed the service with a relevant scripture reading and message.

Our final song was one of hope in Our Lord.

> Let the glory of the Lord rise among us
> Let the glory of the Lord rise among us
> Let the praises of our King rise among us
> Let it rise...[8]

Need I mention that the flyers that were handed out to all attendees also had the Lord's Hand upon it as well. I had been searching through scriptures to perhaps find something on the lost or saved or even grace. Well, what I finally settled on was in the book of Matthew (my son's name) Chapter 5 (the fifth month, the month of May) and I lost my firstborn on May 4th, Matthew on May 6th, and my grandmother on May 8th, hence the "Blessed be" verses. The Lord clearly placed everything together consecutively.

From the love of God's Spirit in the sanctuary to the love of my church family downstairs, the flow continued as they served in abundance an amazing and plentiful feast. My relatives and friends were all truly blessed. Several individuals came over to me, not believing my strength but it was entirely through Jesus that I was persevering.

The full memorial service from beginning to end was soaked in the Lord's anointing. I felt like I was on a cloud, just floating along, and it occurred to me that I was undoubtedly resting upon the Lord's Hand. I may have appeared to be strong externally when in fact my heart was bleeding. My God had lifted me from there to here, knowing how badly I was hurting. He understood that preferably I would desire a different reality in my life, to have Matthew back, but the Lord had a bigger plan for me, one of which was so concealed that He would only reveal it to me bit by bit. Honestly, I couldn't even predict anything right now, like it or not, I had to trust Him above all things, and believe you me that's not always easy.

With an awareness of final completion and an overflowing heart with no boundaries, my sense of duty to honor Matthew for his Celebration of Life was finished. Instead of the finality of a funeral, as I had mentioned before, I wanted all those who attended to accept my faith in believing that my son was with Jesus. It was my sole mission to communicate to them how God is truly right there when you need him, in the darkest of valleys, He is indeed with you. And now my own personal path, my passageway of healing continues.

As soon as I got home, the confirmation of that new path sat very clearly before me. A beautiful surprise awaited me on our front doorstep. Two very caring postal customers had gifted me with a gorgeous rosebush and attached to it was a handwritten note of love, encouraging me to remember my son's life through the beauty of a rose. Precious orange rosebuds adorned this very plant in bloom appropriately named "Perfect Moment." This was the most beneficial time for receiving this stunning gift of life! Thank you, dear friends. Your thoughtfulness is very much appreciated.

Let me rest with this new sensation as I am confronted face to face with euphoria. I have no idea how this garden will look or where to even begin, for that matter. All I know is that this extremely thoughtful gift from a kind couple is most certainly going to be centrally located. I was trusting that everything else would fall into place. Lord, please motivate me to proceed forward on this unknown path of unbelievable proportion, and help me to cope with this profound loss. You are my Rock and my Redeemer, and I cling to as well as lean on You.

Thoughts of the garden set aside for now, I need to concentrate on what lies before me. In two days, it will be "business as usual" as I contemplate going back to work. I can't predict how that task will turn out to be although I do need strength. This is tough. I may appear to be functioning okay, but let's be real. Grief drains the life out of you. No energy... no pizzazz... dark, dull, and dreary. It's truly debilitating.

Prepare me, Lord.

Following my three- week fiasco of highs and lows, the day has arrived, it's finally before me. Dear Lord, stay with me. I am confronted with the chore of getting reacquainted with work. Sure, I remember everything, I know my job very well, but now I'm living with a new normal, one that doesn't include Matthew. As exhausting as my emotions may be, my existence on this earth is crawling forward whether I choose to accept it or not. Blinded by a fog of sorrow, I can't see where the Lord is taking me, but He does have a purpose and for the time being, I will remain oblivious. Things will be revealed to me in His timing, however, at this moment, my only goal is to breathe.

Take a walk in my shoes as I drag my feet onward.

Still riding on waves of shock, but in all honesty, I would love to have Matthew come strolling through that door and give me the biggest hug ever and tell me "Mommy, don't cry," the numbness surrounds me.

Dear God, I ask you to fine-tune my senses. It's almost as if You are pushing me and pulling me all at the same time. I'm weightless as I'm thrown into the frothy waters that are crashing back and forth against the jagged rocks. Once I surrender my thoughts, what comes into view is a dog playing with a toy. He sets it down momentarily, then grabs it again, shaking the toy violently from side to side. Well, I'm that toy! I feel depleted. Just pluck my heart out now and replace it in intervals so that I don't have to grip the full force of remaining steady and unscathed with such an incredible loss. My son abruptly exited my life without warning. Life is unexplainable. God oversees it all and knows what lies ahead while we scramble along one day at a time, and in the middle of sorrow, each minute seems to drag eternally.

So begins my quest to be brave, determined to work hard and accomplish the task of performing a routine that I love. With much tenacity, I held my composure. I didn't want anyone hanging over me, thinking that I was incapable of doing my job. Yes, it is a lot of physical activity but every so often, I have some verbal interaction with a postal customer. There are a lot of caring people out there on the route, so for now I am going to buckle up, be courageous as well as efficient, and save my crying for a more appropriate time.

I CAN DO THIS...

Ejected into this wild and savage world where I am living my own life, breathing my own breath, walking my own walk, and wishing above all else that I could jump backwards to the way things used to be... (Sorry, not happening).

Driving to New York, I have been on the road since 6am. A couple of hours into the ride, I receive a phone call from a very sleepy Matthew asking me "Are you almost here?" or "What exit are you at?" Beforehand I would give him a certain arrival time and he could count on me to be punctual. We thoroughly enjoyed every moment spent together during our visits. I appreciated the idea of him wanting to be around his momma at least for a little bit, since he was usually busy with friends and I could fully understand that. It was imperative that with the distance of separation, we remain a part of one another's lives.

Matt and I would be riding in the car on another occasion in which I had picked him up from New York to visit us

back home in Connecticut. He would play his style of music and be bouncing his head around, saying "Mom, dance with me" and we'd both act crazy and silly, riding down the road. The dancing part was even more fun when we were dancing in my kitchen on solid ground, just being totally limber and foolish together.

I loved when Matthew had his own set of wheels, something that he was so proud of, his beautiful blue Celica. He would drive in for the weekend and as soon as he got here, he would plop himself down onto the futon in his room and let out the biggest sigh. Priceless! I'm glad that he felt so comfortable here. At night we would have a heart- to- heart in which he would talk about things in his life, and Matt knew that anything he confessed to me would be kept strictly confidential. We shared a mutual respect and at times, I would give him advice while Michael would leave us alone, honoring our privacy as mother and son. It was oftentimes amusing when my son would keep talking late into the night as I got more and more fatigued. I'd let him know how tired I was, and he would virtually keep right on talking. Still a very precious moment no matter how weary I was.

It wasn't until after Matt's passing that I discovered that his nickname was "Hedgehog." He acquired this name from his spikey buzz cut hairstyle. A lightbulb went off when I realized that I had given him a small stuffed hedgehog for Christmas last year and the expression on his face when he had opened it. I remember telling him that I wanted him to have something from me in his car as I had the little yellow salamander which he had gifted me with in my vehicle.

I could now interpret that big grin in the photo that I took of him opening that certain present on our last Christmas together. He rode around with the little hedgehog on his dashboard and now that my son was gone, I really wanted that precious token back, however, currently his car was locked away in someone's garage.

Like a bucket of sadness being tipped over, out pours the physical DAYS that intertwine with one another and then there's the spiritual DAZE that holds you in a domain of numbness. Grief is messy and it's challenging, but despite that, if we reach out to God, He cleanses us, wipes us off and clears our minds. His Light covers the darkness that tends to bind us in fear and sorrow.

Tears are like prayers that cleanse our soul. Crying allows us to become vulnerable, whether it be happy or sad tears, it's like letting your soul become visible.

Bless the Lord, O my soul.

Over the next few weeks, life in general was touch and go as I made my way slow and steady from mailbox to mailbox. At times, I would pull to the side of the road to cry, perhaps call someone just to help me get over that emotional hump. A large part of me remained very much in shock, basically going through the motions. It still doesn't seem real, it can't be real, I wish it wasn't real.

As I continue to press forward...

Miracle moment

Wait a minute... I am travelling up a long dirt driveway to accommodate one customer and when I get to the top, there is a horse trotting over towards me as I turn the mail truck around. One horse racing towards the mailbox. Now if that doesn't grab my attention...

Miracle moment

Skip over to another day. On a mailbox marked "311" (Matt's birthday), I see a weird bug, and another time, there is a praying mantis on that same box.

Miracle moment

A deer crosses my path and stops in the field. It twists its head around and stares at me. Behold, God's beautiful creature.

Miracle moment

I am stopped at another mail receptacle and I hear continuous chirping. I am searching hard for the maker of the sound and when I finally locate it, there before me is a red bird and it stops chirping. It was as if my feathered friend was waiting for me to find it. The house number at that address ended with a "92", Matt's birthyear.

Whispers of miracle moments placed strategically throughout the next several months in such a fashion that they were like personal stepping- stones bringing me forward through life. They each had such a "Wow" factor that it was impossible not to believe that it was all entirely the Lord's handiwork.

Piece by piece ----------- peace by peace

Lord, You entered my spirit so subtly and so gently that it wasn't until later that I could look back in amazement on all of Your Greatness, how splendidly You had pieced together the special celebration for Matthew, honoring my precious son's memory as well as giving You all of the Glory. Lord, as I stepped forward into each new day, You were training my eyes to see so many things, too many to be called coincidences. You were communicating to me through life. I viewed it as if my eyes were being washed off in layers by my tears bringing forth a new clarity, a new vision.

Looking at the backyard going into July...

Where once stood a large cottonwood tree and a circular stone wall became the equivalence of a removed stump and all that surrounded it. Open space to be used to our liking. I always envisioned a future flower garden in that spot but I never in a million years could have imagined that I would become inspired through the loss of my son. As my sadness pools in the depths of my soul simultaneously stirring up the Holy Spirit that has been gifted within me through my faith in the Lord Jesus, I see the garden. I don't visually see the garden with my mortal eyes, there's just bare ground before me, but I do have an insight formulating somewhere within my being, making my hands flow and create something so beautiful that it will stir up life. I don't plan on treating this flower bed as an idol because of my loss, but instead will appreciate it because I want to welcome life and the living. Who would ever have thought that my pain could create something so full of love?

In a whirlwind of energetic activity and heartfelt emotion, Matt's memory garden started to take form. Beginning with a wooden flower box handcrafted by Michael, the framework for this foundation was set. Observe the new location for "Perfect Moment," the lovely gifted rosebush. I found a resin lawn ornament which would be a complimentary accent in front of the roses. It was a figurine of a young boy holding up a jar of fireflies. Through sweat and determination, flowers were added, and a three-tier wall was built including pavers and rocks. The reward of my labor was very sobering as I peered out my kitchen window and began to witness life in abundance, hummingbirds, butterflies, chipmunks, dragonflies, and red birds. At nighttime, I could gaze at the solar "fireflies" from the boy statue. Peace, tranquility, and comfort. Let me be still to cherish and appreciate God's living creatures.

Miracle moment

Picture this… My husband had been parking closer to the garage and I would position my vehicle in front of his on the incline driveway. On one individual day, mine was closer to the garage and it was necessary to move it parallel to the front of the house. Well, within the few moments it took to complete that chore, something miraculous happened. When I walked up the hill headed towards the front door, my eyes zoned in on something quite amazing. A large praying mantis was front and center on the glass panel of the door. You might be thinking, sure, it's just a bug, but perhaps you'll let me explain. You see, last summer, Matthew had been cutting grass in the backyard with his usual precision of straight accurate lines when he came rushing into the house to grab his phone. He had seen a huge praying mantis and wanted to take its picture. Unfortunately, the insect was gone by the time he returned. Well, this memory came flooding back in full stream and I also took note of the precise location of this current insect's landing. Remember when I had shared at the memorial service about the note that my son had left on the storm door at 4:07am deliberately placed at eye level. Well, you'll never guess, or perhaps you already have… the praying mantis was poised in its own glory at that very same spot! Not only that but this occurrence happened right around 5:06pm. Call me a weirdo, but I was noticing the little details that seemed to materialize around me, enough so that those very numbers would attract my attention. My boy died on May 6th, accordingly we have the numbers 5 and 6. Did I get a picture of that special mantis? No, however I do believe that the Lord was granting me a visual for my eyes only, a brief glimpse to feel the connection so that I could embrace this very special episode.

Like the bobber in the water, my emotions dip and swirl...

Lasso in my heart, Oh Lord, because it feels like it has been gradually evaporating. That sensation of numbness is still there. Sure, I have these special miracle clippings, so to speak. I have seen them from time to time, but in all reality, it feels as if my eyes are becoming the new strength of my body right now, except when my tears interrupt my vision. Even so, my heart does seem to be healing. It is crucial that in my present vulnerability, I focus on what is good because once my eyes fill up with the negative stuff, I'll keep on sinking and drown in my own tears. The Lord is here by my side, wiping my every tear away, leading me to keep my focus on Him. At the end of the day, the past cannot be altered and it is darker than the darkness before me, but I'm headed in the right direction. I'm ascending from this bottomless pit as I reach for the hand of Jesus, for He is the only Light to get me beyond this weight of reality. I can draw comfort from His Presence and then be filled with His Peace.

A constant battle resonated in my mind. At times, I dwelled in a sense of peace, knowing where my son was and enjoying as well as appreciating what the Lord kept showing me. Still, there was always the case when the reality of separation would set in, and I would stagger into the darkness, wanting my son back, feeling stuck in my despair, and just plain start feeling sorry for myself. I am human after all and grief has truly thrown me off balance.

With the intermittent special moments, one unique day stands out in my mind. There was an isolated pause during my workday in which I was struggling with a bout of depression. I was overwhelmed with emotional thoughts and after pulling my mail truck over to the side of the road, I broke down and cried. I was missing my son excessively. Giving in to total surrender, I prayed silently "Lord, help me through." Once I regained my composure, I crossed over a small bridge which overlooked a babbling brook. In travelling up the road and back, something caught my eye as I approached that same bridge again. A heron was standing in the water, it was so tall and most definitely the first time I had ever seen such a creature. The tall lanky legs reminded me of Matthew. Lord, Thank You for answering my prayer. Besides being in complete awe with this spectacle, I was filled with joy.

In early August, I arranged a get-together with a few of Matt's friends in New York. I had created a photo album for each individual capturing Matthew's growing years. They were overjoyed and grateful for this personal keepsake. This group then surprised me with a sentimental token, one which immediately brought tears to my eyes. It was the little hedgehog from Matt's car! Without hesitation, (after hugs and blubbering) I seated the little guy right on my dashboard. I felt my boy's presence here in the car. Our visit together was very uplifting, this had occurred on a Friday and there were more delights in store.

On Sunday morning, my vehicle was again parked closest to the garage. The sun was shining through the windows at an unusual angle. After preparing for church, I took my place in the driver's seat and sat there totally mind-boggled. The front windshield was veiled with a fine mist. It resembled a coating of moisture, and I had the pleasure of witnessing a rainbow stretching from the left side to the right side directly over the hedgehog. My thought process was further activated as I imagined a hedge of protection over me, another precious souvenir from God.

Within the next few days, I could attest to observing two more separate rainbows. In addition, I was blessed to see the most amazing sunset outside the hospital window while visiting my ill father-in-law. Unfortunately, Walter had suffered a stroke besides having dementia and other health issues, and he was in this medical facility declining rapidly. I knew this was difficult for many family members, however the Lord blessed us with an opportunity to pray together over him. Sadly, we lost Walter a couple of days later, three months to the day of Matt's passing. Even though we had more grief to bear, I still believe that the Lord once again had His Hand over the entire situation, bringing hope and light to us all, and that Walter was now at peace in paradise. I thank God for the times we did get to spend with Mike's dad.

Perhaps by now you must be thinking, why so many gifts and what is the significance? Being completely honest here, I can tell you that facing the death of someone you love so dearly whether you were forewarned, or it happened unexpectedly, it throws you completely off solid ground. Your foundation is removed, dropping you into a proverbial ocean to sink into the darkened abyss. You have nothing, but when you realize that you have your faith in God, all things become possible. The Lord gives you just what you need, Our Father Himself becomes our floaties, our flippers, our goggles, and even our actual air tank. As we submit to Him, He is our Coach, our Teacher, our Encourager, and ultimately our Savior. It's not like we get the waters of the sea completely parted for us. The Lord parts it in moderate proportions. You see, as we swim and release what we don't need, we are building our "faith" muscles. When all is said and done, we are doing the hard work ourselves, it's not handed to us. It is through the struggles along the way that we are propelled forward to heal our hearts, basically teaching us how to swim. Yes, there will be scars while tending to the sorrows and the measures of our pain, it's all part of the process. Eventually it all becomes our own personal testimony, one which we can use to help others with their journey because we are coming from a place of experience.

I do have to admit that those very first moments following Matthew's death were the most difficult. Like a form of separation anxiety, your body becomes coated with a layer of shock. A new reality is set before you, waiting for you to accept the fact that you will not be physically able to see your loved one again. And that in and of itself is a hard pill to swallow, metaphorically speaking. While we are on that topic line, choosing to drink alcohol or take drugs or even overindulge with food, all of these options tend to cover the first emotion, making it that much harder to heal, adding a top coat if you may. In the beginning, my primary care doctor did offer me a sedative to make it easier for me to cope, but I declined. Usually, there is a common thread that when you need help, you seek a doctor and receive a prescription for your ailments, hence you go to the local pharmacy. Imagine this… you choose to skip the doctor visit, go directly to the drug store and have a conversation that goes something like this:

Customer: Excuse me, I have a need for a mourning kit, do you sell them in this store?

Pharmacist: Oh yes, we have a few assortments available and they can be purchased right over the counter. If you follow me, they are down this aisle… Hmm, okay, here they are. (picking up a box) This one is our top seller, it has the highest dosage and it includes everything needed, along with a variety of drugs, a very popular brand I must add. (pointing to a second package) With this medium toxicity selection, you also have your necessities but this particular one offers unlimited alcohol inside, this one certainly is a crowd pleaser. Our third variety comes in a low impact version. Some people favor this one because it comes with an overabundance of food, a real smorgasbord. Oh, but then there's this one last kit hidden here in the back, quite often it's the least chosen one. The only thing in that box from what I've been told is a single bible. So, which one would you prefer?

The choice is yours and it's a choice that will not only shape your future but it will also affect all others in your life as well. For me, I choose not to have anything that will cloud my mind or take me emotionally off solid ground, so please hand me the bible.

The Lord continued to cover me in His care as my husband and I took a small vacation to Maine and Canada. We saw clouds shaped like a lobster and an airplane. While in Canada, we encountered Matt's name on three occasions. I certainly couldn't ignore the obvious, meaning the man at the deli, the youngster at the café, and the name etched into the sidewalk equaling Matt, Matt, and Matt! Lord, I thank You repeatedly for You are always with me. It was quite the relaxing and pleasurable trip. We just had one final stop on our way back through Maine, to catch a glimpse of the alpacas. Matthew had loved these furry little beings.

As my emotions begin to fishtail...

Something about the rain, it seems to encourage the tears to flow. But why should my mood be orchestrated by the weather? So here we go again...another crying spell. Why is it so hard to lose someone you love? When I first found out that I had lost Matthew, I had immediate provisions for a torrential downpour, my own personal storm where the flooding would begin making way for gushing waters that would toss and spin simultaneously. Welcome to my world. Yes, other family members were dealing with the pain in their own manner, but I was in no condition to be of aid to them because I was striving to survive as well. Call me selfish, but I needed to assist myself first. Just because I was dependent on the Lord did not mean that I wasn't going to feel the multitude of emotions along with the physical aspects of grief. I'm not exempt, I am human after all. Oh, but how oftentimes I felt as if my life was simply not my own. I was merely being slid forward at a gradual pace day in and day out. Bring forth the light and shine down on me.

With appreciation, may we admire the beauty of the autumn leaves...

As I moved further and further away from that day of major impact, and again unaware of the people who might still be praying for us, with a splintered heart I was starting to gain ground. The Lord was my Rock. My existence was profoundly different, and the tears were still there, but just not as heavy. My burden was indeed being shared. As it is written in Galatians 6:2, we are to bear one another's burdens, helping each other to fulfill God's law. Many caring souls were most definitely raising me up both in prayer and in kindness.

A couple of mini excursions away from home was great medicine on my path to healing. On one such day when our schedules permitted the perfect opportunity, my daughter and I took a day trip to Newport. It was so breathtaking by the ocean watching the waves crash, picking up seashells, having solitude moments with our own thoughts, and then coming back together for quality time appreciating the serenity of peace. We savored a delicious meal at a fine restaurant and found ourselves filled with silliness and laughter. It was almost as if we left our sadness by the water. We were both missing our Matthew intensely, and our lives were forever altered without him. Clearly, it was a necessity for Tiffany and me to be on this special trip filled with time well spent together as family. She is my only living child and I love her dearly.

As the leaves float to their new destination...

One bizarre occurrence that stands out in my mind took place during an average workday. It was a common procedure to bring customer's packages to their door, so when the cause came that this action was required, I parked the mail truck and prepared to depart. However, something caught my immediate attention. Through the front windshield, I witnessed a single leaf spiraling down towards the ground, lifting into the air again, and then completing its descent directly by my driver's side window. It was amazing how it ventured downward but even more shocking was the leaf itself. I opened the door and picked up that piece of God's creation. To my surprise, the leaf had three holes in it, placed in such a pattern that it reminded me of a Mickey Mouse symbol. In years past, I had taken both of my children to Disney World. This made me smile, it was such an unexpected yet brief interruption out of my normal routine.

Let us sweep into the holiday season where the leaves have stopped falling, the trees are barren and the snowflakes will soon cluster, allowing a shift to occur. With a renewed yearning to see my boy, my heartache becomes raw once more. Matthew spent many a Thanksgiving and Christmas with family here in Connecticut. What was starting to mend on the inside was becoming torn wide open on the outside. While I reflected on special memories, feeling silent and somber, wisps of light started to collect in my brain. Our Lord was interceding my thoughts by giving me a wonderful idea, one that awarded me a new perspective, allowing me to use my love for Matt to pour out positive energy.

For the record, I hadn't touched anything in Matt's room. A small decorated Christmas tree remained intact since last year. I had no desire to take it down. Sitting in there, I would often weep and at other times, I would get on my knees and pray. As this new "lightbulb" of an idea formulates... here goes. I've decided to decorate that little tree with all sorts of items that Matthew loved. Imagine the ornaments that I would discover... bagel and lox... four-wheeler... stack of pancakes... skateboarder... N.Y. ... a fish catching a man (something silly) ... a cell phone... a crab... a lobster... even delicate feather angel wings. Amongst these trinkets were a nativity ornament and a cross with the words "Child of God."

Sad tears followed by tears of joy and peace emotionally knitted together in the presence of one Christmas tree...

This may all seem mundane, but in a sense, it was drawing me closer to my son. There really is no perfect way to heal but this was my way. Whatever it was going to take, I was living, breathing, and working hard to get through this grief process. I assure you, there was no pattern, no rhyme, and no reason for this never-ending task. It was like being stuck inside a snow globe with my emotions floating lifeless, sometimes shaken, sometimes settled, looking out at the colors around me, longing to be near them but unable to be released. In order to relieve the burgeoning cascade, labor and effort were highly necessary. Again, this wasn't to be in my timing, it would be in God's.

I did my best to stay upbeat over the upcoming weeks. There were still some occasional waterworks over the holidays but who could expect anything less? I loved my son dearly and was missing him something awful. The sadness was like having a Band-aid over my heart, it would begin to cure and once the bandage was ripped off, a raw open wound would remain. I do have to say though, the hurt wasn't nearly as bad as the earliest days of my loss, so I could expect that recovery would be inevitable. Somehow, in some way, the Lord was bringing me through and I'm certainly not going to question the One who is Our Almighty Father.

Let Him Reign...

I was gently drifting forward one blessing at a time. On top of that, one very dear family donated a beautiful angel of lights in Matt's memory to a place of Christmas festivities. This token of generosity was truly one such blessing which lifted my spirits.

As a family unit, we celebrated Day One of the new year with light and words of love for Matthew. I had printed out a poem from the computer and a BMW advertisement covered part of the words unexpectedly. Was I surprised? No, Matt loved his cars, and those covered words, it turned out to be something special pertaining to him. From our hearts to yours, Matt, we love you.

Enter February...

Being a mail carrier, it is quite common for me to deliver items of all shapes and sizes. Imagine my surprise when I myself received a personal parcel addressed from New York. I don't often get packages so to me this was quite heartwarming. What was even more special were the contents. Inside I found an adorable stuffed hedgehog with its arms wrapped around a Happy Valentine's Day heart as well as a container of chocolates. A couple of Matt's friends had seen it in a store and thought of me. How kind and considerate of these dear girls. This really made my day special.

Oh, and remember Matt's Christmas tree... with each coming holiday I set in motion a routine of interchanging the ornaments accordingly by adding hearts, shamrocks, eggs, and the like, you get the picture.

One wintry morning towards the end of February, I was leaving the house and made the most unusual observation, not only unusual but what looked completely impossible. Lord, You have gifted me with sight but what I'm seeing right now... it's bringing tears to my eyes. It's beyond amazing, and only You could make this one possible. There in complete view on top of my car was frost pointing to the sky appearing to be like spikes. Well, of course I would start to cry because it reminded me of Matthew's spikey hair. This image could only belong to a time as brief as this and I knew it was one that I would never behold again.

... Incoming miracle moment...

Talk about feelings of aggravation turning to pure joy. My daughter and I were subjected to an episode of rare proportions. Here's what happened... Tiffany and I were having a conversation on the phone when she started to give me an attitude. I became annoyed, choosing not to listen and hung up on her, placing the extension on the kitchen table. I sat there, mulling about her behavior. After a few minutes, I heard my daughter's voice saying "hello, hello?" My cell phone was on the screen saver, no black screen like when you dial someone. I answered her and stated that I hadn't dialed her. Tiffany replied that she hadn't called me either. What? Looking back at my phone, thoughts began accumulating and I started to laugh. She asked me what was so funny. I informed her that the picture on the screen displayed Matthew and I felt that he was letting us know how foolish we were to bicker. He really was always the peacemaker. We both got a good chuckle out of it. Thanks, Matt. Point taken.

As I secured a comfortable spot on my healing path, I felt confident enough to reach out to help others. My stance on this matter came to light when I chose to write encouraging words in a card to my ex-husband, David. He was Matthew's father after all and together we were Matt's parents. He lost our son also, and it was the right thing for me to do by reaching out with compassion and forgiveness. In addition, through Tiffany, I was able to message a prayer for her dad whenever he would need surgery or medical procedures. The Lord was guiding me to be the encourager. Let me assure you, time does not heal all wounds, but it was certainly helping.

With anxiety and anticipation both in the running, fighting to be first, God intercedes with peace. Picture a rosebud when it opens to its full potential and one is faced with indescribable beauty. Well, that describes this very moment for the Lord has adorned the sky with magnificent color, His Glory shining through a stunning sunrise. I could not ask for a more welcoming presence on this day, however bittersweet it may be, for today is my son's birthday.

Yes, Matthew's birthday is upon us and we will be celebrating this one without him. Add this to the many firsts that we've already faced in his absence, such as Thanksgiving, Christmas, etc. It all aches but we try to stay positive anyway. So, with the light of this day, it is my desire to "gift" my son. Having said that, I have purchased a decorative blue bench to be placed under the arbor near Matt's memory garden. I am trusting that this will bring even more tranquility as I watch for living things in the garden and view it from a different perspective. Besides, the kitchen window limits my perception, as appealing as it may be. Likewise, if I sit still on the bench long enough, I could perhaps witness a hummingbird in mid-flight heading towards the feeder. Future flashes of bliss… peace… and joy.

Clearly, the Lord was beckoning me to step forward into this gorgeous daylight, allowing me to abandon my earlier vigilance, to toss it aside, sight unseen. To my delight, my phone had two loving messages waiting to be heard, one from Tiffany and the other from Tami. Both my daughter and my sister were checking in on me. Their thoughtfulness was very well received, and I responded to them happily. I do love my family! With the fullness of a tender heart, I have great aspirations for today. In addition, that choice seat really does compliment the yard beautifully.

We got on the road shortly after 8am, with a quick stop at a local grocery store. I ran inside and grabbed a rose and a helium birthday balloon. Upon cashing out, the cashier noticed it was a singing birthday balloon, but unfortunately the device wasn't working. No big deal, I was in a hurry, and I really wanted this specific item. It had cute comical faces on it, something sentimental that reminded me of Matt's silliness. Maybe my actions seemed a little quirky, but in my mind, I was on a mission. Besides that, there is no perfect cookie cutter way to get through grief, and for that matter, there's no symbolic recipe either, so on days full of tears, perhaps the ingredients get a little soggy. In my opinion, on this day the ingredients are just right.

Special items in car, off we go...

Let's jumpstart this trip with some family love as we make our first connection. Here we have Mom, Tami, her son Jordan, and his daughter Ariana. Behold, car number two as we start developing our own mini caravan.

Next stop: meeting Allen and Diane. Riding with my brother and cousin, I relinquished my responsibility of driving. This works out perfectly because I can be totally honest with my feelings, both good and bad, while speaking with a compassionate listener, one who is also a mom. Personally, I would love to see my son's smiling face at the other end of this road trip, but instead the plan will be to reunite with his friends and his dad. We will all be sharing company at the spot where Matthew is buried.

Having a fascination for numbers, whether forward, backward, what have you, they tend to jump out at me. My attention seems to be drawn to them, so think of me casually looking at my phone to unexpectedly see that it's 11:11am. From there, I glance up and notice that we're approaching cubicle number 11 at a toll booth. (Mind you, my brother is driving). Upon calling my daughter, I shared these tidbits and learned that she and her husband, who are travelling farther behind us, have just passed exit #11. Honestly, can this really be? Add to that the fact that today is the 11th of the month. Okay, now I genuinely feel that we are in the right place at the right time and I also believe that the Lord is all around us, directing our entire path. One might say that this is all completely coincidental, PERHAPS, but I lean towards undeniably REAL.

At the cemetery, I sat in the car for a little while, gathering my senses while letting the others go over to his grave first. Subconsciously,

I felt that this was Matthew's resting place for his physical body and that his spiritual body was with Jesus. Upon preparing myself to join the others, I noticed that David and Grandpa Joe had just arrived. Together, Mike and I went over to extend a quick hello to the two of them. After that, I carried the one single rose to the gravesite. This beautiful flower was the same color as the roses that had bloomed in Matt's memory garden last year. With careful thought, this token of love represented something special that I had transported from Connecticut to here, connecting my heart to my son's.

Throughout our lives, whether it be good times or bad, our Lord is always faithful. He places people and circumstances in the right place at the right moment and bear in mind, it's not always through our personal way of thinking. Currently, surrounded by these very dear friends here in New York as well as my relatives, I feel very blessed. In addition, Pastor Lane has called to check in on me. I appreciate his thoughtfulness. Presently, I am encircled by a lot of caring individuals between family and friends.

I felt an impulse to have Michael collect the balloon from the car. It was time, now that everyone was present. After regaining possession of the brightly colored inflatable, I gently tapped it. To my amazement, the tune of "Happy Birthday" filled the air and to think that it wouldn't work earlier. With watery eyes, I began to vocalize the musical notes as the others joined in, together lifting our voices to sing this common birthday lyric to Matthew, as I released the balloon sending it off to Heaven.

We love you, Matt...

Shortly thereafter, Tiffany sat on the ground near his gravestone and played the song from <u>Casper</u> called *"Remember me this way"* sung by Jordan Hill.[9] [10] I knelt beside her, hugging my daughter as we both cried. God, we miss him so much. We used to watch this movie together when they were both younger and I reminded Tiff of a funny part which made her laugh. Lord, please freeze-frame us in this special moment that my daughter and I are sharing. Let us hang on to these beloved memories.

Connecting hearts, connecting love...

I had a desire to gift my son's colleagues with something of significance, so I brought bracelets with me. Knowing how much Matthew loved children, I had purchased these handwoven items to benefit an orphanage overseas. They were received with warmth and one close friend of Matt's gifted me with a personally handwritten poem. It was a beautiful tribute written about Matt and I was honored that she wanted me to keep it.

An atmosphere of goodwill permeated the air as we all dispersed our separate ways.

Following a quick lunch out with friends and family, the immediate travelling party from my brother's vehicle made our way over to the docks, one of Matt's old places of hanging out. It was nice to see Debbie, my former sister-in-law there. We spent a short time reminiscing. Originally, we had wanted to send off sky lanterns, but the area was far too windy for that to happen. That's fine with me, I'll save mine for another day. In any event, it was a thoughtful gesture.

In preparation of our ride home, setting aside the fact that I was totally drained, I chose to disregard my brother's GPS. I knew my way back to the highway. I had driven this same path back and forth for many years while visiting Matthew. Bottom line... robotic voice, move over. I have my own directions.

I kept feeling queasy during the trip, perhaps a little anxiety overall. A mixture of sensations enveloped me. Suddenly, I became alert to my whereabouts. Following the second toll booth heading back, we would soon be going through a tunnel area. When my kids were little, we would at the beginning of the tunnel start saying "wee" and try to carry our voices out until light shone again, basically at the end of the tunnel. Tiff and Matt would have to take a few breaths in between. So... here in Allen's car, the four of us will do just that! I sent a message to Tiffany about it and she would do the same. Both her and Sean had left a little while later than us. Upon arriving home, I looked up to the sky and there was my completion of a perfect day. A ring around the moon! Thank You, Lord for holding us in Your Hands and guiding our steps on this day. I am also thankful for being a part of this awesome family and having such loving friends. God bless them all.

An occasion arose towards the end of March in which I was approached to fulfill a unique favor for the church. In all actuality, it was a special request which proved to be a hidden blessing once every detail was revealed. Imagine my surprise when I found out that they wanted me to wear a costume of a pink hedgehog. Absolutely! With everything that was going on in my life right now, this was an honor as well as a great distraction from my various thoughts. Me, the one who was commonly known as quiet and shy, was being asked to step out of my comfort zone. How could I say no when this was for a great outreach? It was for Friendship Day at our church and we were opening arms to one and all. As I waved and motioned to passersby, the invitation was out there. Come into our church and feel the love of Christ. My heart was flourishing with Christ's love as I embraced this gift of serving with such enthusiasm. Many thanks to the Lord for answering this mother's silent prayer — connecting me with Matthew but also advancing me along on my journey to restoration.

As we roll into early April...

Through the trials and tribulations of my thoughts and emotions, I continued to "collect" several more amazing miracle moments, more blessings to forever cherish in my mind.

Another such moment occurred on our way to see a movie. Mike had dropped me off at the door of Panera Bread while he parked the vehicle. Once I placed the order, the cashier posed a question asking me if I was interested in donating to some sports organization. Yes, of course I would, and was then given a choice to choose a wrist band in red or blue. For me, I'll take the blue one, thank you. I teared up after looking at it, for there before me were the words "I (heart) Mom" in white letters. Seriously?! In addition to that, after our meal, we went to see the movie _Heaven is for Real_.[11] A few days earlier, Tiffany and I had seen this very same film. We were both quite moved by the true- life story of a young boy named Colton Burpo and his visit with Jesus. As we both cried, a much- needed beautiful bond was formed between the two of us, initiating more restoration into our relationship. My daughter and I could better comprehend each other's hurt in a totally new light. Seeing this movie once again in the company of my husband was just as moving. I have to admit that I left that theater feeling an even deeper love for Christ.

As we welcomed family at our home for Easter dinner, I felt a touch of despondency with the awareness of Matthew's absence. He is missed so very much by all of us. On a separate note, I portrayed the part of an angel in an Easter play. This was a big feat for me, to have the ability to memorize my lines with the haphazard way my brain was functioning, but I knew that the Lord was helping me. In addition, there was a great time of fellowship with my fellow castmates. It was a great diversion in this season which became an even bigger blessing when my daughter drew closer to Christ. Praise God!

Where has the time slipped away to as we approach the one-year anniversary of Matt's passing...

Bittersweet and tender are my heart strings as the anxiety starts building up just before that day. Invariably, it's a day of personal remembrance. May 6th. It's here and it's upon us. One year ago, today... sure, I could sit here and be outright stagnant, wallowing in self- pity, then state the obvious— Matthew died. Reverse that and I could consider the other selection which has hope and peace attached to it— Matthew went to be with the Lord. I prefer to believe the latter because it allows me the freedom to cry, to embrace my sadness, and with this I have the hope of seeing my son again. I wouldn't want it any other way. I'm still going to experience my messy moments, my blank stares, and broken thoughts. That's normal. They're all part of my journey and it's the way things are right now while I steadily ease myself forward with my healing. The Lord lets His Presence be known repeatedly that He is always there and I am in His Fold. He has strengthened my faith and given it wings. He has given me breath to get up and face each morning head-on. To thank the Lord for His guidance and support, I must pay it forward, so to speak. Through my experience, I have understanding and compassion to walk alongside others on their grief journey. Taking this into account, I propose that today we all honor Matthew with something that he loved doing, whether it be fishing, car cruising, listening to music, being outdoors, even his pleasure of eating. My desire is to encourage others to think of my son with smiles and laughter. Matt would want that for everyone.

Between us, in remembrance of Matthew, Mike and I have chosen to go out for a nice dinner. The sequence of events that followed gave me confirmation that we were exactly where we were meant to be. The flowers outside of the inn were in full bloom, and in the garden was a statue of a young boy. During our dinner, a couple of songs played reminding me of my son. The meal itself was delicious. Following our departure of the restaurant, we spotted some deer in the field, all adding to the tranquility of peace and love which rested in my soul as I held Matt's memory deep in my heart.

(A day of reflection is sandwiched in between)

May 8th – one year ago, my very dear grandmama passed.

Upon completing my postal job for the day, Tiffany met me in the parking lot. She gave me a ride to my car which was hysterical because it was only a short distance away. Seriously, I could have walked. We both silently watched from her vehicle observing an oriole flitting in and out of some white blossomed trees. The color contrast was breathtaking. It was accompanied by a precious span of healthy conversation between mother and daughter. More importantly, Tiffany is my only future lifeline here on this earth. As we give ourselves permission to heal, we discover that we have been gifted to open our hearts to a love that has no reservation and at the same time, we possess a deeper compassion for one another.

We took a quick spin over to a nearby pharmacy. A wire metal bird sculpture caught my attention because it reminded me of a heron. I was so captivated with the colors that I purchased two of them, one in blue and the other in purple. I surmised that this would add a nice accent to the memory garden. After departing separate ways, I reached out to my mom. When my dad answered the phone, he relayed the word that she had gone to visit Gram's grave.

After pulling in at the cemetery, I found the destination to be vacant. Subsequently, I felt a nudge prompting me to drive to Grandma's house which was only a few minutes down the road. There on her property, I saw my mother, my aunt, and a few cousins.

They were walking around the grounds, preparing to spread Gram's ashes. Being here brought back many fond memories. It was on this day that I learned that Gram had a heron that visited at the pond behind her house and she had named him George. Interesting how this really resonated with me, because there was a young boy named George on the mail route whose mom had consoled me in the early days of my loss. A full circle was becoming very apparent. We were each distributed a portion of the cinders, and as I released mine, I became excited and filled with joy. I began throwing the "sand" up into the air, letting some of it land on me. I truly believed that Grandmama was with us all at that moment and I felt lighthearted with a new sense of freedom.

Ashes to ashes and dust to dust...

The very next day, while scurrying around the mail route, I picked up an outgoing letter addressed to a George Dunn. With some evaluation, while approaching the delivery for a local pharmacy, the same place where I had bought the two herons, I pondered about writing a book. In silence, I asked the Lord if the timeframe was complete for this project. I also thought about that letter, George being the name of the heron and Dunn meaning done, finished. In answer to this idea, I witnessed white blossoms before me floating to the ground. Thank You God for Your response. Dearest Lord, I have heard You and I have obeyed.

It's a fine line between the light and the darkness when facing the challenges of grief, one path allows fear to keep you stagnant, while the other one leads you to hope and joy. We all have choices to make at the crossroads of decision, and that very choice will form and shape your future. I chose to give myself to the Lord in complete abandonment. To get acclimated to a new lifestyle without Matthew around was very difficult, but I was trusting in God anyway. That hurt is always going to be there but as I move further along on this laden path, I have come to realize that I am focusing more on the hope of seeing my son again once I get to Heaven. Therein lies the hope with a future, and it is with my eyes brimming with tears that I place my faith on the One who created me, the One who brought me out of the sludge and the muck that I was trudging through. He has brought me to a new place of love as well as mercy and I have been transformed into a new creature. I am born anew with the power of the Holy Spirit surging through my breath and my veins, transporting me from the past to the present. The past is gone and there it shall remain. I have a new spirit that desires to reach out and help others who are hurting.

My journey through this process is just that— my own. By reaching out in faith, the Lord has without a doubt been right there close to my side. Now, I can't say each person's path with Our Almighty Father will be the same for everyone. The Lord spoke to me in a language that was unique for me, something that I could relate to and understand. He knew that I loved nature and had a penchant for numbers. As an individual, this was my connection with the Lord. For others, they will have different ways of communicating with Our Father. All in all, God gives us just what we need when we need it, but in His timing. Besides that, it is a part of life that we are forced to experience tests and trials which ultimately make us stronger so long as we persevere. However, in the long run, that perseverance leads to a personal testimony. I can't even imagine where my life would have been, what paths I would have chosen, feelings I would have denied and suppressed if I hadn't reached out and grabbed onto the Hand of the Lord. He pulled me out of the darkest of trenches, He kept me afloat in the ocean of sorrow, and then He placed me on solid ground. I'm certainly not perfect and I don't claim to be a know-it-all. Nevertheless, the Lord accepts my every flaw and loves me anyway. He is my firm foundation and I am proud to be a child of God. With grace, Our Lord and Savior placed all the right people on my path. Bottom line, He gave me hope. Do I still encounter miracle moments? Absolutely! I've seen a heron fly by me in slow motion, witnessed the beauty of the brightest red bird as well as the intimate details and colors of a blue jay, and the list goes on. God's creation is beautiful. It took me a long time to realize that our loved ones are so deep in our hearts that they are always with us and we take them wherever we go. Our eternal connection is love everlasting through Christ. I am thankful for my journey, not for the fact of losing my son, but for the growth in me and the opportunity to help others. Perhaps there is someone out there reading this book right now that needs the guidance of Our Father. I encourage you to reach out to a local church, or even open a bible. The Hand of Jesus is outstretched, ready and waiting, and once you grab hold of it....

Believe and Let Him Reign.

Epilogue

In closing… I can't say that I healed in one year by any means. I'm just sharing how the Lord carried me through that first year, with my every emotion hanging out on a sleeve. Perhaps some feelings in the beginning may have seemed extreme and unfair to others, but this is how I felt, no sugar-coating anything. When Matthew died, I was forced to make a choice, fight against everything that was happening around me or give in to the Lord in total surrender. By placing my heavy burdens upon Jesus, the suffering didn't subside however my pain became more bearable. It was an agonizing experience to identify and work through the many faces of grief, however despite my loss, I gained so much more in return. As I began to truly know the Lord's Presence, it was then that I could acknowledge the beautiful personal relationship that was forming between us. I am not only a child of God but I am also His friend.

It is written in the Bible that God will take our tragedies and turn them around for His good. While we are in the midst of all of the chaos of our own reactions, we can't see beyond our own selves, but unbeknownst to us, it is at this time that the Lord is challenging us and teaching us to lean on Him, because the final result will be for His Glory. How could I ever predict the many miracle signs that the Lord opened my eyes to see, miracles that let me know without a shadow of a doubt that for one, God is real, and secondly, that my dear son is indeed in Heaven. In addition to that, I have developed an even deeper and healthier relationship with my daughter, Tiffany.

Lastly, there is the forgiveness of every person who may have hurt or wronged me as well as forgiving myself for any misconceptions. It is that final release that frees your soul, and allows you to become a better person, one who is more like Jesus.

In a gentle whisper, God had been calling my name. I was baptized in water in 2010, declaring my belief in Jesus before others. Right here, now, today, I could feel the Lord's Spirit surrounding me completely. As you all know, this individual passage of my life started off with an unforeseen storm, a host of rough waters and torrential rains. With the Lord's help, I was able to prevail. In my younger days as a baby, I learned to crawl which later led to walking and running. By God's grace and mercy, I was learning how to swim but not just in any water, it was in and through His Living Waters. I was submerged into the hard work, gasping and paddling to save my soul, to a point where I could glide and float in His Peaceful Waters. Now I can't say that every moment in my life is untouched or unscathed by negative issues and problems. Obviously, I love the peaceful waters as much as the next person, however it's unrealistic to believe that life is just that, filled with mounds of only goodness and serenity. Reality tells us differently.

Through Adam's first bite of the forbidden fruit, sin entered the world. Adam already had a close relationship with God, his Creator until temptation intervened. On display in front of him was a choice, obey God's command or satisfy his own needs with Eve's prodding. With God, there was truth, trust, and provisions, things that were often unseen. However, there before him was the other selection, the apple. It was perfect and it was enticing and above all, Adam could see it, yet God had ordered him not to partake of that certain tree. The first man already had access to everything that God had made. He was extremely blessed. Unfortunately, temptation does look beautiful but beware of the hidden fingers behind it waiting to snatch you away from the Lord. The gratification from temptation is only fleeting. It can lead to feelings of guilt, shame, and unworthiness. Thankfully, when you become a child of God and accept Jesus as your Lord and Savior, He understands that we are not perfect, that there are weaknesses as well as temptations and we sometimes make mistakes. We can't hide anything from Him, including our nakedness, but through our trust and faith in Him, we are able to persevere. Furthermore, we need to remain mindful of our actions, admitting our sins before the Lord and asking for His forgiveness. He is the strength which stands firm whenever we are weak, and His Strength is available to all who believe in Him. Jesus has said "No one can come to the Father except through Me". (John 14:6). We need to remember that God loves us no matter what we have ever done throughout our lives and He meets us right where we are. He desires to change our lives so that we can reach our potential for His Glory. Be humble and allow God, Our Healer, Our Savior, Our Comforter, Our Redeemer, Our Rock, and so much more, to walk with you daily. Not only is His Hand waiting to take yours to walk alongside of you, but His Arms are wide open, inviting you to come in for a welcoming hug of LOVE.

frost on car

cloud that looks like airplane

cloud that looks like lobster

an amazing sunset

rainbow inside car

Matt's memory garden

Matt's Christmas tree

Friendship Day

Acknowledgements

First and foremost, I thank God for being the author of my life and for being so profoundly present in bringing me through this journey from the darkness to the light. Lord, I pray that this book touches many lives, as people open their hearts to You, giving You all the Glory.

Much gratitude goes out to the entire Inspiring Voices team for their assistance in making this book a reality.

Thank you to my husband Michael for your understanding when I would get up in the wee hours of the morning to write thoughts down. Honey, you're the best.

Thank you to Edie for your awesome artistic skills in teaching me about color and shadows. Your assistance helped me as I brought this book cover to life.

Thank you to my daughter Tiffany for showing me how to use spell check and grammar. Sweetie, you saved me a lot of time.

Thank you to Pastor Lane, Dave, and Holly for your tips on footnotes and endnotes and computer skills respectively. It was very helpful.

Thank you to the couple of individuals that I shared bits and pieces of my writing with. You encouraged me immensely.

Thank you to Peggy and my neighbors, Mike and Jean. The three of you were pioneers throughout the entire process.

A huge thank you to the many people who supported and prayed for this book. You all have been waiting a long time for this.

To all of my family, friends, and acquaintances, I love you.

God Bless You All.

Notes

1   Darlene Zschech and Hillsong team, *"Savior King"*, Andrew Crawford, Joel Houston, Reuben Morgan, recorded March 18, 2007, Acer Arena, Sydney, Australia, Hillsong, track number 14 on *"Savior King"*, released July 1, 2007, CD.

2   *The Karate Kid*, directed by John G. Avildsen, Christopher Cain, performed by Ralph Macchio, Noriyuki "Pat" Morita, Elisabeth Shue, produced by Jerry Weintraub, distributed by Columbia Pictures, 1984, film.

3   Nickelback, *"Far Away"*, Chad Kroeger, Ryan Peake, Mike Kroeger, Daniel Adair, recorded January-May 2005, Mountainview Studios, Abbotsford, British Columbia, track number 4 on *"All the Right Reasons"*, Roadrunner Records, 2006, CD.

4   Chris Tomlin, *"How Great Is Our God"*, Chris Tomlin, Jesse Reeves, Ed Cash, produced by Ed Cash, track 3 on *"Arriving"*, sixsteps/ Sparrow, released September 21, 2004, Album.

5   Jo Dee Messina, *"Heaven was needing a Hero"*, track number 1 on *"Unmistakable Inspiration"*, Curb Records, released on November 9, 2010.

6   English poet and Anglican clergyman John Newton, *"Amazing Grace"*, written in 1772, published in 1779, Hymn.

7   Darlene Zschech and Hillsong team, *"Savior King"*, Andrew Crawford, Joel Houston, Reuben Morgan, recorded March 18, 2007, Acer Arena, Sydney, Australia, Hillsong, track number 14 on *"Savior King"*, released July 1, 2007, CD.

8   Holland Davis, *"Let It Rise"*, Holland Davis, track number 7 on *"Healing Word"*, released 2002, Album.

9   Performed by Jordan Hill, *"Remember Me This Way"*, written by David Foster, Linda Thompson, produced and arranged by David Foster, Courtesy of 143 Records/ The Atlantic Group, featured in 1995 film *Casper*, soundtrack.

10 *Casper*, directed by Brad Silberling, performed by Christina Ricci, Eric Idle, Cathy Moriarty, Bill Pulman, produced by Colin Wilson, production

company: Amblin Entertainment, The Harvey Entertainment Company, screenplay by J.J. Abrams, Deanna Oliver, Sherri Stoner, 1995, film.

11 Heaven is for Real, directed by Randall Wallace, performed by Greg Kinnear, Kelly Reilly, Connor Corum, Margo Martindale, Thomas Haden Church, produced by Joe Roth, T.D. Jakes, Devon Franklin, production company: Roth Films, distributed by TriStar Pictures, screenplay by Randall Wallace, Christopher Parker, released April 16, 2014, film.

CPSIA information can be obtained
at www.ICGtesting.com
Printed in the USA
BVHW081629310721
612760BV00002B/121